THE CATHOLIC THEOLOGICAL SOCIETY OF AMERICA

THE CATHOLIC THEOLOGICAL SOCIETY OF AMERICA

A Story of Seventy-Five Years

CHARLES E. CURRAN

Paulist Press
New York / Mahwah, NJ

Library of Congress Control Number: 2020952445

ISBN 978-0-8091-5574-3 (paperback)
ISBN 978-1-58768-973-4 (e-book)

Published by Paulist Press
997 Macarthur Boulevard
Mahwah, New Jersey 07430
www.paulistpress.com

Printed and bound in the
United States of America

CONTENTS

FOREWORD

Readers interested in Catholic theology in North America over the past eight decades will find this short book of significance primarily because of the story it tells, but also because of the author who relates that story.

The Catholic Theological Society of America officially came into being at a meeting held at the Commodore Hotel in New York City in June 1946. There, over one hundred representatives from U.S. and Canadian seminaries and theologates, all Roman Catholic priests, ratified the constitution of the new society and articulated its mission: "Its primary object shall be to promote an exchange of views among Catholic theologians and to further studies and research in Sacred Theology. Its secondary object shall be to relate theological science to current problems." As the following chapters recount, since that inaugural meeting, at its annual conventions and through the work of its members, the CTSA has sought to advance its mission across eight decades marked by dramatic growth, changes, and challenges for the Church, for North American society, and for the field of Catholic theology and its practitioners.

Today the CTSA is described as "the principal association of Catholic theologians in North America, and the largest professional society of theologians in the world," and its demographics differ strikingly from the white, male, clerical cohort who attended that first meeting in New York. The society's thirteen hundred plus members are lay, ordained, and religious; women and men; they represent many cultural backgrounds and social locations; and they teach or work in an array of academic, pastoral, and institutional settings. Yet despite these changes, the contours of the organization and its mission—"to promote theological research in the Roman Catholic tradition that is attentive to contemporary problems faced by the Church and the world"—continue to reflect the vision and commitments of its founding members.

Recounting the CTSA's seventy-five-year story herein, in his trademark forthright and no-nonsense style, is a scholar who, for over three-quarters of that story, has quite literally been there. Reverend Charles E. Curran, of 433 Rocket St., Rochester, New York, was among seventy-five new members inducted into the Catholic Theological Society of America at its fourteenth annual meeting, held in Buffalo, New York, in June 1959. Ordained a priest for the Diocese of Rochester just one year earlier, the twenty-five-year-old Curran joined the CTSA having just completed his licentiate in sacred theology at the Gregorianum in Rome. He would go on to complete two doctorates in sacred theology in Rome and return to the United States in 1961 to begin a remarkable, six-decade-plus career as a priest, scholar, teacher, and influential public figure in the field of Catholic moral theology.

The years spanning Curran's induction into the CTSA in 1959—the same year that Pope John XXIII announced the Second Vatican Council—and this book's publication in 2021 have been awash in the dramatic events, transformations, conflicts, and—to echo the Council's words—the joys, hopes, griefs, and anxieties of the diverse peoples and communities of the Catholic Church in North America. During those sixty-two years, Curran has played his own, at times controversial but unquestionably significant, role within that larger narrative: as a prolific researcher, writer, and publisher; teacher and mentor to generations of students and colleagues; and a conscientious public voice on contemporary issues in Catholic theology and ethics.

Charlie has been, as well, a tirelessly engaged and contributing member of the Catholic Theological Society of America. As the society has experienced its own changes and challenges, he has served it in numerous leadership roles, including as its twenty-fifth president in 1970. In 1972, the CTSA officially recognized his contributions to the field of Catholic theology by bestowing on him the inaugural John Courtney Murray award.

By example, Curran has also taught scores of theological cohorts what it means to be a dedicated CTSA member. Over the years he has been a model institutional citizen (never missing either the business meeting or the Women's Consultation in Constructive Theology session); a friendly and gracious community builder (inclusive, post-session cocktail hours in "Charlie's room" became such a tradition that, rather than forego it due to 2021 pandemic restrictions, a virtual re-creation of the event was incorporated into the seventy-fifth annual convention's official program); a supportive and wise mentor to his fellow members; and for CTSA leaders, a reliable, go-to colleague willing to help advance whatever might be needed by or contribute to the society, its members, and the CTSA's theological mission.

These same virtues inspired Charlie to write this book, working with Paulist Press and the CTSA leadership to publish it for the occasion of the seventy-fifth anniversary of the founding of the society. Taking note of the fact that two previous efforts to commission an official history of the CTSA had, for different reasons, never come to fruition, Curran decided he might be able to write something that would be useful. His contribution, he hastens to remind his readers, is neither an official nor an exhaustive history of the society; its author is neither a trained historian nor an archivist. This is, rather, a theologically and institutionally focused "story of 75 years," written from the perspective of an active "participant-observer" who has witnessed the vast majority of that history firsthand.

In this volume, then, Charles Curran offers his readers, and the CTSA, a signature gift, emblematic of the innumerable gifts he has bestowed on so many in his priestly, teaching, scholarly, and collegial ministries over the years. As one among the multitudes who have benefited from every one of those ministries—beginning in the 1970s as a student in the classrooms, offices, and chapel of Catholic University's Caldwell Hall, up until today—I am especially honored, on behalf of everyone in the society, to thank Charlie for his generosity, and to present this, his latest gift, to you.

Christine Firer Hinze
Fordham University
CTSA President, 2021–22
March 17, 2021

PREFACE

In preparation for the fiftieth anniversary of the Catholic Theological Society of America (CTSA), the board of directors commissioned a church historian to write the history of the society. Unfortunately, the work was never done. In preparation for the sixtieth anniversary, the board commissioned a different church historian to write the history, but the result was the same—no history was written.

In preparation for the seventy-fifth anniversary, the president-elect asked me to present a paper at a special evening session celebrating the anniversary. I assume that I was invited because I was the president for the twenty-fifth anniversary in 1970 and have been a very active member of the society for sixty years. I can recall missing only one meeting in all these years.

I set about preparing for that presentation in January 2020 and was able to devote myself full-time to the proposed paper since I was not teaching that semester. Also, since I was sheltering in place for over two months, I was able to devote almost all my time to this project. As I worked on the paper, my curiosity grew as I reviewed what had transpired at the annual conventions in the seventy-five-year history of the CTSA. It gradually dawned on me that I might have the interest and time to write a relatively short history.

There was, however, a major problem. I am not a historian by training or profession. I have always been interested in and written on the historical development of my discipline of moral theology, but I was writing as a moral theologian, not as a historian. As I said to one colleague, I write about the history of moral theology, but I do not do archives. In reading over many of the annual publications of the Proceedings of the Catholic Theological Society of America, I became aware that the annual minutes of the business meetings in the Proceedings provided the members with the basic realities of the internal life of the society. The president and other officers updated the membership on what was going on in the work and life of the CTSA. There is no doubt that archival research would explain in greater detail and depth what transpired in the life of the CTSA, but the annual business meetings provided the basic story of the life of the society.

In thinking and reading about the seventy-five-year history of the CTSA, I was puzzled by the fact that on two different occasions the board had commissioned historians to write the history, but no history was ever written. It seemed to me that there was more than coincidence about the failure of these two attempts. Historians could readily be frustrated by the fact that in this case one also had to have a good knowledge of the theology that evolved in the life of the society. Training as a historian was not enough to write a history of the CTSA. Something more than superficial knowledge of theology was also needed.

I came to three conclusions. First, I could do an adequate and basically accurate history of the CTSA based on the knowledge of the life and actions as made known to the membership at the annual meetings and at the same time discuss the actions and resolutions taken by the members at these annual meetings. I would also bring to this work my own role as a participant observer of the meetings of the CTSA beginning in 1962, two years after I joined the society. Second, on the basis of the past experience, it would be very difficult to find someone to write the history. Third, it would also be very difficult for an individual to write the history and find a publisher willing to print such a book. Prospective buyers for such a volume are very few. Not all and probably not even close to a majority of the members would be interested in purchasing the book. One would hope that the libraries of Catholic institutions of higher learning and other theological libraries would be interested. There could also be a number of other interested readers. The bottom line, however, is that the volume would probably never be published without some financial help from the CTSA. The CTSA board itself recognized the need for some financial subsidy coming from the society when the project of writing a history on the occasion of the fiftieth anniversary was first proposed, and a committee went into action in 1990 (1991, 210).

With all this in mind, including the need for some funding from the CTSA, I contacted Christine Hinze, the president-elect, who invited me to give the paper at a special session of the 2020 convention on the seventy-fifth anniversary of the society. I told her that I already had rough drafts of the first two chapters and a week later again sent her a rough but readable draft of chapter 3. I figured that a book of four chapters would probably come to about 150 published pages I also explained to her much of the background already described in this introduction. She quickly gave me an enthusiastic, positive response and said she would consult with others in the presidential line of the CTSA about the project.

I have purposely chosen the title *The Catholic Theological Society of America: A Story of Seventy-Five Years* as the full title of the volume. Since I am not a professional historian, I did not want to use the word *history*. In addition, it is not "The Story." My own background and perspectives are bound to color what I have written. *A Story of Seventy-Five Years* is thus the most appropriate subtitle for this book.

The first chapter of the book treats the origins of the CTSA. Some background information on the status of theology and

Catholic higher education helps to elucidate the understanding and role of theology. Philosophy was the most important discipline and subject in Catholic higher education before 1950. Other disciplines in Catholic colleges, such as sociology and economics, started professional organizations before the theological society. The seminary was the home of Catholic theology, and the approach was pastoral more than academic. Many courses in theology were taught in Catholic undergraduate programs, but the approach was catechetical rather than academic. The fact that a person was an ordained priest or a vowed religious was often all that was required for one to teach such courses. The idea for the Catholic Theological Society of America ultimately came out of the theology faculty of the Catholic University of America (CUA). Faculty members from CUA were the founders of the CTSA in 1946. CUA at the time was the only graduate school of theology in our country. Note that graduate programs, not only in philosophy but also in other disciplines, had come into existence much earlier.

The easiest way to structure the volume is to discuss the three twenty-five-year periods of the CTSA, thus forming chapters 2, 3, and 4. I toyed with the idea of finding another way to outline the book but could not find a logical approach. There is no doubt that the first twenty-five years showed very well the change and development in Catholic theology occasioned by the work of the Second Vatican Council (1962–65). But there is no such unifying theme in subsequent years. The reaction to *Humanae vitae* heavily influenced the 1970 to 1995 timeframe, but there were many other factors, as well. The pluralism of issues and concerns is even more present in the third twenty-five-year period of the existence of the CTSA. As a result, it seemed that the chronological approach to the outline of the book is not only the easiest but also the most logical way to structure the volume.

As mentioned, the story of the CTSA involves both historical and theological aspects. Such an understanding gave structure to chapters 2, 3, and 4. The first part of each chapter deals with the internal life of the CTSA, and the second part deals with the theological aspects, including both methodology and content topics and issues.

A further word about the theological content of this book is necessary. It does not and really cannot cover all the theological discussions or papers that have taken place at the CTSA conventions during these seventy-five years. One comparatively small volume cannot do justice to the theological record of the CTSA. Another more significant limitation about the theology discussed here comes from the fact that, in subsequent years, there were close to fifty sessions at each convention, sometimes with two or more papers at an individual session. The *Proceedings* have generally published just the plenary sessions, often with responses, and the presidential addresses. Only brief excerpts or abstracts of the papers given at the breakout sessions have been published in the *Proceedings*. Thus, the *Proceedings* themselves contain only a small number of the papers given at the conventions. Even if one were to cover all the presidential and plenary papers, each would receive one or two sentences in the book. Such a book would read like the phone book. I have selected what I think are the most pertinent papers, with special attention to presidential addresses and papers given by the best-known Catholic theologians.

Two comments about style are in order. To facilitate the reading of the book, I have put references to the *Proceedings of the Catholic Theological Society of America* in the text, giving the year and the page numbers, for example (1984, 120–23). Second, I was happily surprised by the fact that, for the most part, even from the very beginning, the *Proceedings* have not used ecclesial and religious titles. As a rule, I have followed this same approach.

The current president, María Pilar Aquino, the president-elect, Christine Firer Hinze, and the entire board have enthusiastically supported this endeavor after I first brought it to their attention.

THE CATHOLIC THEOLOGICAL SOCIETY OF AMERICA

It is most appropriate to have the story of the CTSA published in conjunction with the seventy-fifth anniversary of the existence of the CTSA. The seventy-fifth anniversary was scheduled to take place at the 2020 convention, but that was postponed to 2021 because of the COVID-19 pandemic. In many ways, writing this book has been truly a labor of love. I have enjoyed my sixty years as an active member of the society and have made friends and acquaintances with many of my fellow members.

As mentioned, I am most grateful for the support of the board of the CTSA in publishing this volume. I discovered in my research that Paulist Press had published the early volumes of the CTSA *Proceedings*. Paulist Press also published the twenty-volume series *Readings in Moral Theology* that I coedited and edited from 1979 to 2020. I am most grateful that Mark-David Janus, CSP, the CEO and publisher of Paulist Press, was willing and anxious to publish this volume and have it available before the scheduled June 2021 CTSA meeting. Once again, I have benefited from the professional and careful work of my editor, Donna Crilly.

This year marks the thirtieth anniversary of my coming to Southern Methodist University (SMU) as the Elizabeth Scurlock University Professor of Human Values. This chair was funded by the late Laura Lee and Jack Blanton in honor of Laura Lee's mother. I have found SMU to be a congenial and challenging academic home. Colleagues, students, librarians, and administrators have supported me in my teaching and research. The one person most helpful in the preparation of this book is my administrative and graduate assistant Lisa Hancock. She has provided friendly and most efficient help while juggling many other familial and academic responsibilities.

Chapter 1

THE ORIGINS OF THE CATHOLIC THEOLOGICAL SOCIETY OF AMERICA

The Catholic Theological Society of America held its first meeting in 1946. To understand better the origin of the CTSA at this time, the historical context is helpful.

HISTORICAL CONTEXT

The Catholic Church in this country in the first half of the twentieth century was primarily an immigrant church. The concern of the Church at this time was precisely taking care of its own members. The intellectual life was not the primary concern of the Church.

The first professional academic society in the United States was the American Catholic Philosophical Association. It began in 1926. The society published a scholarly journal, *The New Scholasticism*, from 1927 to 1989. In 1990, the name of the journal was changed to *The American Catholic Philosophical Quarterly* and is still published today.[1] In 1925, the Jesuit scholastics of the philosophy department at St. Louis University began publishing *The Modern Schoolman*, which, beginning in 1928, was published as a quarterly and later became a faculty-edited publication of the philosophy department of that university. In 2012, the name was changed to *Res Philosophica* with the goal of publishing in all areas of philosophy, both Catholic and non-Catholic.[2]

In the late 1930s, Catholic academics and colleges paid significant attention to the papal social encyclicals. In 1938, the American Catholic Sociological Society began and in 1940 first published its review, *The American Catholic Sociological Review*, with the primary intention of applying the principles of Catholic social teaching as found in the encyclicals to the American scene. This society at its height had nearly five hundred members but did not want to cut itself off from the broader discipline of sociology. A few years later, a similar group of academics founded the American Catholic Economic Association and published the *Catholic Economic Review* with the same purpose as the sociological group. In light of Vatican II's development, both groups changed their names and the names of their journals and moved beyond just the Catholic parameters. The sociology group in 1970 became the Association for the Sociology of Religion and its journal was called *Sociology of Religion: A Quarterly Review*. In 1970, what had been the American Catholic Economic Association became the Association for Social Economics.[3]

Other Catholic academic associations and new scholarly publications occurred about the same time. In 1939, the newly formed Catholic Biblical Association began publishing the *Catholic Biblical Quarterly*. The Canon Law Society of America began in 1939, and the School of Canon Law of the Catholic University of America (CUA) began publishing *The Jurist*. The Dominican fathers started the *Thomist* in 1939, a scholarly review of philosophy and theology, with more emphasis on philosophy. The first scholarly publication in theology was *Theological Studies*, begun by the Jesuits in the United States in 1940. Catholic journals existing at that time tended to be primarily pastoral, such as the *American Ecclesiastical Review* and the *Homiletic and Pastoral Review*. Some more scholarly articles did appear in these journals, but the primary purpose was still pastoral.[4] As noted, only in 1946 did the Catholic Theological Society of America come into existence.

What explains these facts? The primary concern for this study is the fact that scholarly Catholic associations and publications began much earlier than the theological association and scholarly theological publications. Why was philosophy the area of the earliest academic associations and publications? As mentioned, the Catholic Church in the nineteenth and early part of the twentieth century was an immigrant Church. There was much prejudice from many other Americans about this immigrant Church. The leaders of the Catholic Church strongly emphasized that Catholics could be good Americans and insisted on assimilation. But Catholic education in general was the one exception to this assimilation. The feeling was that Catholic education was absolutely necessary to preserve the faith of Catholics in this country. The Catholic school system began in the nineteenth century and continued growing to the time of Vatican II (1962–65). Most parishes at the direction of bishops insisted on the presence of the Catholic elementary school. Many times the school building itself was built first. Catholic religious women staffed the growing elementary schools. Religious sisters, brothers, and priests staffed the high schools. The ready availability of such "cheap labor" was most important in the growth of Catholic elementary and high schools. Part of the reason for the decline of such Catholic schools after the late 1960s was the great decline in the number of Catholic religious.

From 1786 to 1849, forty-two Catholic colleges were founded, but only twelve of those have survived. One hundred fifty-two Catholic colleges for men started between 1850 and 1900 and another seventy-two began between 1900 and 1955.[5] Nineteen Catholic colleges for women began before 1905, and by 1955, 116 were founded.[6] However, the early men's colleges were a far cry from our contemporary understanding of a college. From their very beginning, these colleges contained both secondary and collegiate students in a seven-year curriculum. Only in the early 1920s did the preparatory departments separate totally from the colleges, which then followed the ordinary American four-year pattern.[7]

On the first page of his history of Catholic higher education, Edward J. Power sets out the primary purpose of all Catholic education: "From the outset, all schools from primary through college grades were preoccupied with preserving tenets of faith and with teaching policies ensuring the allegiance of Catholic people to their Church. A good end could shape its own means."[8] Catholic higher education was shaped to achieve a primarily religious end. The college was intimately joined to the pastoral arm of the Church. Intellectual formation was subordinated to the preservation of the faith and moral formation. Such a distinctive purpose made the Catholic college quite different from and even opposed to the non-Catholic college.

One example of Catholic opposition to other forms of higher education in the United States is found in the inaugural address (spring 1949) of Father Hunter Guthrie, SJ, the thirty-fifth president of Georgetown University. The arrogant tone of the speech, on an occasion where representatives from many secular and non-Catholic institutions were present, only heightens the hostility of his remarks. The newly inaugurated president of Georgetown paints a very negative picture of humanity at the midway point of the twentieth century. The contemporary human being is a finer piece of machinery but much less a person than his horse-and-buggy prototype. Humanity is floundering today because it has lost its ultimate orientation. The blame falls on the contemporary American university, which has persuaded modern humanity to live without God and convinced us that all design, purpose, and meaning "are to be found in the squirrel cage of his [sic] own Ego." In the land of the free, many schools by policy, others by law, are not permitted to disclose all aspects of reality. Without revelation, we cannot know what is important, and we cannot attain certain knowledge. Opinion and not truth becomes the final product of American university education. All these contradictory opinions are so much philosophical balderdash for one who has seen the Promised Land of total reality.[9]

One might think the distinctiveness of the Catholic college came from theology, but that was not the case. Philosophy, specifically Thomistic philosophy (often called neo-Scholasticism), was the primary factor distinguishing the Catholic college in the United States at this time. In his 1879 encyclical, *Aeterni patris*, Pope Leo XIII mandated the philosophy of Thomas Aquinas as the official philosophy of the Catholic Church. The Catholic Church strongly opposed the Enlightenment and much of modernity. Leo used Thomistic philosophy to address the problems of the modern world. Thomistic philosophy showed how reason could prove the existence of God and that faith was compatible with reason. The new 1917 Code of Canon Law for the Universal Church required that professors of the sacred sciences were "to teach the method, doctrine, and principles of the Angelic Doctor." Church authority imposed the teaching of Aquinas on all Catholic institutions of higher learning.[10]

The cultural crises that occurred after the calamity of World War I were reinforced subsequently by the economic depression and the rise of totalitarianism. Thomistic philosophy was the vehicle by which Catholic intellectual institutions could address these modern problems.[11] Philip Gleason, now the emeritus professor of history at the University of Notre Dame, referred to

5

this era from 1920 to the early 1960s as "the Catholic Renaissance."[12] Thomistic philosophy served to criticize the problems of the modern world. This Catholic Renaissance involved an intellectual and cultural Catholic approach. In this ethos, one can understand the origins of the American Catholic Sociological Society and the American Catholic Economic Society mentioned above. This Catholic Renaissance gave further support for Thomistic philosophy that had been imposed by Pope Leo XIII and subsequent authoritative Church pronouncements.

Catholic colleges required all students to take a large number of courses in Thomistic philosophy, but Thomism involved more than just a large number of required courses. Thomistic philosophy gave a meaning and a unifying force to the whole curriculum. Its aim was to bring about a distinctive Catholic culture, which permeated the entire college. It should be added that individual students did not always understand this integration, but it was the aim of Catholic higher education.

Why did Catholic theology not play the primary role of integrating and directing Catholic higher education? After all, these Catholic colleges at this time also required a great number of courses in Catholic theology, but often called just religion. These courses, however, were primarily catechetical and pastoral in orientation. The teachers themselves seldom even had an advanced degree in theology. It was thought that priestly ordination or religious profession was all that was needed to teach these courses. The Jesuits and Dominicans made some attempts to pursue a more academic approach to these religion courses, but their attempts did not have that much effect. In the mid-1950s, a small group of Catholic teachers of religion founded the Society of Catholic College Teachers of Sacred Doctrine, which in 1967 changed its name to the College Theology Society. This society came into existence in response to the need, recognized by most people on Catholic campuses, for theology to be taught from a much more academic perspective. Catholic educators generally recognized that these religion courses were not in keeping with the academic nature of what the college tries to be.[13] Thus, theology could not play the role of organizing and directing the curriculum and approach of Catholic higher education in the period before 1960.

Before the 1960s, institutions of Catholic higher education handed down the traditional wisdom of the past and saw themselves in opposition to secular higher education. The leading figures in administration and faculty were priests, sisters, and brothers of the religious communities who staffed most of these institutions. Even in the late 1950s, laypeople often felt like second-class citizens on Catholic college campuses. Change came from several directions. After World War II, Catholic colleges expanded with the return of war veterans and an upwardly mobile Catholic population. These colleges continued to grow in the 1950s and 1960s. More laypeople, even some trained in non-Catholic institutions, had joined the faculties of these growing institutions. In this context, many people then began to call for a greater professionalization in the academic nature of Catholic higher education. The Second Vatican Council (1962–65) influenced many in Catholic higher education to support the move out of the ghetto and the acceptance of the approach of existing higher education in the United States.[14]

In the summer of 1967, twenty-six leaders of Catholic higher education in North America, meeting under the auspices of the American Region of the International Federation of Catholic Universities, issued the "Land O'Lakes Statement." The pertinent part reads as follows:

> The Catholic University today must be a university in the full modern sense of the word, with a strong commitment to and concern for academic excellence. To

perform its teaching and research functions effectively, the Catholic university must have a true autonomy and academic freedom in the face of authority of whatever kind, lay or clerical, external to the academic community itself. To say this is simply to assert that institutional autonomy and academic freedom are essential conditions of life and growth and indeed of survival for Catholic universities as for all universities.[15]

The home of Catholic theology before Vatican II was not the Catholic college but the seminary or theologate whose purpose was pastoral—the training of future priests for their ministry.[16] In such a context, there was little emphasis on the academic nature of theology. Until Vatican II, the textbooks in theology in the United States were in Latin, and the authors were mostly European. In 1961, I began teaching moral theology at St. Bernard's Seminary in Rochester, New York. The assigned textbook was the Latin manual of the Austrian Jesuit Hieronymus (Jerome) Noldin (1838–1932). His successors in Innsbruck brought out new editions as time went on, but these editions almost always involved new Church documents or revisions of canon law.

The professors in these seminaries and theologates did have doctoral degrees in theology, mostly from European institutions, especially the pontifical universities in Rome. The vast majority did not see themselves as academicians. As a rule, these professors seldom wrote books or even articles in theology. There was no encouragement or any incentive to write scholarly articles or books. Recall that it was only about 1940 that the more academic theological journals of the *Thomist* and especially *Theological Studies* came into existence.

What about the role of the Catholic University of America, which had been founded in 1887? Graduate theology was supposed to play a very important role at CUA. CUA conferred nine doctoral degrees in theology from 1895 to 1908, but no more until 1917. From 1917 to 1935, the university conferred only thirty-four doctoral degrees in theology. One of the primary reasons for the lack of strong theological scholarship at CUA was the fact that most seminary teachers in the United States received their doctoral degrees abroad. During World War II, CUA gave many more degrees because it was impossible for people to study in Europe. As a result, from that time forward, CUA began to become a greater force in the doctoral teaching of Catholic priest theologians in the United States.[17]

This historical section has showed why the professionalization of Catholic theology as illustrated in a professional society of Catholic theologians was so late coming on the scene in the United States.

THE BEGINNING OF THE CTSA

The founding of the CTSA took place in the light of this background.[18] There had been a number of discussions about starting such a society in the early 1940s. For example, at a banquet for theological students at Catholic University in the spring of 1941, such a society was seriously talked about. Considering this somewhat enhanced role of the School of Theology at Catholic University during World War II, it was the logical place to play a role in founding such a society.

After a board meeting of the *American Ecclesiastical Review*, which was published at Catholic University, Father Eugene Burke from the university's School of Theology insisted on the need for such a society. His two colleagues at that October 1945 meeting, Fathers Edmond Benard and Joseph Clifford Fenton, strongly agreed. These three also agreed that another colleague,

Father Francis J. Connell, the professor of moral theology at CUA, was the logical person to take the lead in the formation of this society. Father Connell enthusiastically agreed and scheduled and chaired several meetings with Burke, Benard, and three other CUA colleagues. Connell asked then-Archbishop Francis Spellman of New York and then-Archbishop Edward Mooney of Detroit, the head of the National Catholic Welfare Conference, for approval of the project, and they readily agreed. Spellman graciously invited Connell to call the preparatory meeting in New York. Connell scheduled such a meeting in the hall of St. Paul's Church in New York for January 27, 1946, to plan for the new society. Thirty-eight priests were present at the meeting. The group elected Connell as chair and Fenton as secretary.

Connell appointed a committee of seven to draft a constitution and bylaws for the association. It was agreed to have the first meeting of the society in New York during the week of June 23, 1946. The chair appointed a committee to make arrangements for the June New York meeting. The committee itself held a further meeting in New York in April and sent out letters to all the seminary and theological faculties in the United States and Canada, inviting all teachers of theology to this first regular meeting of the Catholic Theological Society in New York in June. It is interesting to note that they explicitly wanted to include Canadians in the society.

The first meeting of the Catholic Theological Society of America began on Thursday, June 29, 1946, with a Mass of the Holy Spirit at St. Patrick's Cathedral with an auxiliary bishop of New York "offering" the Mass and Cardinal Spellman presiding. Note the protocol of such celebrations at this time where the cardinal presided but did not "offer" the Mass. Spellman welcomed all in attendance and personally met each one of them. The sessions of the convention itself were held at the Commodore Hotel. The nominating committee prepared the following slate of officers: Father Connell as president, Father Gerald Yelle from Canada as vice president, Father Fenton as secretary, and Father James E. Rea of New York as treasurer. Four board members were also nominated. All of these were elected unanimously. At the business meeting, Connell as president appointed three different committees — on admissions, on current problems, and on research and publication. The committee on current problems reported to the board on current topics that might be addressed at subsequent meetings.

Significant actions at the business meeting included the following. The society petitioned the Holy Father for the definition of the doctrine of the Assumption of Mary. The pope had earlier asked bishops and theological faculties for their advice on this issue. The meeting discussed giving awards to members for their theological publications and contributions but thought such awards would be more significant if sponsored by a member of the hierarchy. Cardinal Spellman agreed to sponsor the award and gave a sum of money to support a monetary gift accompanying the award. Thus, the Cardinal Spellman Award was to be given annually to one of the members for outstanding achievement in theology.

The business meeting also approved the constitution of the society to be known as the Catholic Theological Society of America. "Its primary object shall be to promote an exchange of views among Catholic theologians and to further studies and research in Sacred Theology. Its secondary object shall be to relate theological science to current problems." This secondary object reflects the American penchant for a more practical approach to things. There are two types of members — active and associate. Active members are those who are or have been actively engaged in the promotion of studies and research in sacred theology. Associate members are those who wish to identify themselves with the aims of the society. No mention is made here that the active members must be priests. This was just assumed since priests were the only ones who were theologians at that time. History will show how gradually membership became open to all those who hold the appropriate degrees or their equivalent. The constitution goes on to describe the meetings of members, the officers and board of directors, the committees, and other matters. The bylaws, among other things, maintain that Robert's Rules of Order shall govern the deliberations of the society where it does not conflict with the rules of the society or of the sacred canons.

The three papers read at the first meeting of the CTSA give a good understanding of the approach to theology at that time. The paper of William R. O'Connor of St. Joseph's Seminary, Dunwoodie, the seminary of the Archdiocese of New York, was entitled "The Wisdom of Theology" (1946, 21–33).[19] There is more interest in theology today than might have first appeared. Many today are disillusioned with the Enlightenment in the speculative order and the crass materialism in the practical order. In the Middle Ages in the universities and in monastic schools, theology provided a unifying approach to learning and to the living of the Christian life. In those days, theology was truly the queen of the sciences. Theology, with the gift of the Holy Spirit, today can overcome the disillusion that many experience. The *Summa* of Thomas Aquinas can bring about a systematic understanding of theology and how the Christian life should be lived today.

O'Connor here disagreed, without saying so, with the approach taken by the leadership of Catholic higher education at this time. Catholic colleges made Thomistic philosophy and not theology the unifying and directive science for the curriculum and aims of Catholic higher education in this country.

There is a more fundamental question to raise. At this time, the theology in existence was not really Thomistic at all. The two major branches of theology in U.S. seminaries were dogmatic and moral theology dealing with doctrine and life. Their textbooks were all in Latin and were usually called manuals, many of which had been written decades ago by Europeans but had been brought up to date. A 1935 study from CUA mentioned six manuals used in dogmatic theology in the U.S. seminaries, but the vast majority used that of Adolphe Tanquerey. Five different manuals were used in moral theology, with the manual of Jerome Noldin used more than any other. A study by John Boere in a master's dissertation at Catholic University written in 1963 pointed out the three top dogmatic theology manuals were those of J. M. Hervé, Tanquerey, and the Spanish Jesuits. Eight of over seventy seminaries used the *Summa* of Aquinas. Noldin again was the most used textbook in moral theology. Thus, only a comparatively few seminaries used the *Summa* as their textbook, despite O'Connor's claim that the *Summa* itself is of primary importance for theology today.[20]

The manuals of theology themselves did not really follow the method and approach of Aquinas. The manuals of dogmatic theology followed the method of starting with a thesis or proposition and then proving it. The process or method of proving the thesis was basically the same in all the manuals. The first step was to explain the meaning of the terms in the thesis, followed by the adversaries, the teaching of the Church, the theological note or importance attached to such teaching, the proof from Scripture, the proof from tradition, the teaching of theologians, and theological reasons supporting the thesis.[21] Notice that the first and primary proof came from the official teaching of the Church. Such an approach was a far cry from the approach and method of the *Summa* of Aquinas.[22]

The manuals of special moral theology were often based on the Ten Commandments, explaining in turn the sins against each of them. The approach of the *Summa* was entirely different. The *Summa*'s purpose was not to determine what acts were sinful and the degree of sinfulness. The *Summa* approached special moral theology using the virtues and not the commandments.

Two related questions arise: why did many at this time think the manuals were Thomistic in their approach and method, and why did all the directives from the papal magisterium calling for a Thomistic method and approach not influence these works? One cannot do any more here than simply state some of the reasons for this. The manuals had been in existence for a long time, some for over fifty years. They gave a primary role to official Church teaching. No one ever accused them of heresy or of going against the teaching of the Church. In the process, they probably did quote Thomas Aquinas more than any other Catholic theologian. Thus, they were considered to be Thomistic.

The paper of Francis Connell of CUA, "The Catholic Doctrine on the Ends of Marriage," begins by citing the April 1, 1944 decree of the Holy Office (1946, 34–45). The Holy Office later changed its name to the Congregation for the Doctrine of the Faith, but its purpose was to safeguard Church teaching on faith and morals. The primary end of marriage is the generation of offspring. All other ends are secondary and subordinate to the primary end. Such a teaching requires internal and external acceptance, which is called religious submission. To deny this teaching is a grave sin of disobedience and rashness. The document is rightly condemning the work of Father Herbert Doms. Connell points out that procreation as the primary end of marriage provides the main argument for the sinfulness of contraception and divorce. Here and elsewhere, the paper does appeal at times to the teaching of Thomas Aquinas, but the primary reason given is the authoritative teaching of the Church as found in the document of the Holy Office.

The primary purpose of procreation in marriage means that the rhythm method is *per se* illicit, but *per accidens*, rhythm can be accepted when there are sufficient reasons for use, such as financial stress or serious danger of health. This teaching on the primary end of marriage rejects any possibility that future investigation will alter this teaching. The reality is that two decades later Catholic theologians strongly challenged this teaching and dissented from the Church teaching on contraception repeated again by Pope Paul VI in the encyclical *Humanae vitae*. Connell's paper well illustrates the primary role in theology of the teaching of the papal magisterium in this time frame.

The third paper at the 1946 meeting was from Father Joseph Bluett of the Jesuit theology school at Weston, Massachusetts: "The Theological Significance of the Encyclical *Mystici Corporis*" (1946, 46–60). *Mystici Corporis* was the 1943 encyclical of Pope Pius XII. Bluett maintains that *Mystici Corporis* calls for a treatise *De Ecclesia* (ecclesiology) whose emphasis and proportions will differ very widely from those we have known. In the existing manuals, *De Ecclesia* is a part of fundamental theology whose purpose is to show that Christ formed a Church that carries on in time and place the work of the risen Savior. Now, ecclesiology can no longer consider itself just to be a work of fundamental theology. There will still be a need for this role of fundamental theology as the logical beginning of theology. However, at the end of the whole theological process, there should be a truly dogmatic theology of the Church in which all dogmatic theology attains the crown that *Mystici Corporis* has made for it.

Bluett recognizes this task will take effort and time. But in reality, it would be very hard to rewrite the manuals that had been in existence for many years. The updating of the manuals by subsequent editors over the years would never take such a drastic change. As noted earlier, basically the same manuals were being used in the 1950s as had been in used in the 1930s. In fact, it was only with Vatican II that the manuals were finally phased out.

This short first chapter has described the origins of the Catholic Theological Society of America. The antecedents of the formation of the society help to explain why and when it came into existence. In addition, the constitution and bylaws of the society indicate what its purpose and function was to be. The contents of the very first meeting also give a good idea of the state of theology at that time in 1946.

Chapter 2

THE CATHOLIC THEOLOGICAL SOCIETY OF AMERICA, 1947–1970

This chapter will discuss two different aspects of the development of the CTSA during this time frame—the internal life of the society and the theological content found in the papers presented at the annual meetings.

INTERNAL LIFE OF THE SOCIETY

This section will consider the internal life of the society in terms of what occurred at the convention meetings, especially in terms of the business meeting itself. The format of the meetings was constant throughout this period with a few variations. The business meetings of the society were very much like the business meetings of any society and included the election of officers. The nominating committee presented a slate for president, vice president, secretary, and treasurer, and three members of the board of directors. By the very nature of their office as secretary and treasurer, the holder of these offices served for a number of years to ensure continuity. The committee nominated one person for each office and three for the board. For over twenty years, this report was always unanimously accepted by the membership.

The 1962 annual meeting (the seventeenth) passed a resolution that "ordinarily the vice-president will be nominated to succeed to the presidency." Only at the 1967 meeting in Chicago did the nominating committee present two candidates for the office of vice president. By then, the former president *ex officio* became a member of the board of directors for two years, and the committee proposed four names for the two new board member positions (1967, 347–48).

Two other types of meetings were involved in the internal life of the society. The board of directors met in the fall. For many of the early years, they met at the Redemptorist House in Washington. In addition, the Committee on Regional Meetings made a report at the 1954 convention urging the establishment of such meetings and even suggesting possible regions. The president should designate a provisional chair for each of the regions with the charge of trying to bring such regional meetings into existence (1954, 39, 240–42). Some of the regional meetings thrived. For example, in the twenty-third convention in 1968, the committee reported on regional meetings in both the New York and Baltimore–Washington regions that met in the fall and the spring. The Chicago regional meeting was held in December. Some regions that had been active before were now inactive (1968, 285).

The story of the internal life of the CTSA is found in the business meetings at the annual conventions. This section will discuss three significant facets in the internal life of the society in this time frame—Church-related aspects, membership, and leadership.

Church-Related Aspects

The CTSA from its beginning saw itself as intimately connected with the institutional Church represented by the hierarchy.

The first meeting in New York in 1946 occurred after Cardinal Spellman approved the idea of founding the society as such and invited the society to meet for the first time in New York City. In the next few years, the CTSA asked permission of the local bishop to meet in his diocese. At the early meetings, the local bishop on the Tuesday morning presided at a Mass of the Holy Spirit. Often, the local bishop also used the occasion to address the society, welcoming the members to the diocese and giving at times even a more substantial address. Early on, the president celebrated the Eucharist on the second morning for the departed members of the CTSA. With regard to the Eucharist, individual priests celebrated private Masses, which were set up either somewhere in the convention hotel itself or in a neighboring church. The first item in the proceedings of the early meetings was a full-page picture of the local bishop. It became customary to confer honorary membership in the society on the local bishop. To this very day, the local bishop is invited to speak to the society at its first session and welcome the members to the diocese, but the local bishop no longer celebrates or presides at the opening Mass.

The 1952 convention spelled out in greater detail the selection of the Cardinal Spellman Award winner. The selection committee consisted of three members, the president and the previous two immediate predecessors as president. Two factors are to be considered in selecting the nominee: (1) outstanding written contributions to theology during the calendar year preceding the giving of the award; (2) general outstanding service to theology, not necessarily within the calendar year, with written work being primary but also including distinguished teaching and service to theology. It is preferable that the nominee fulfill both criteria, but the committee may decide that only one of the factors is sufficient (1952, 48–49). Note that the proposal for the criterion for the selection had been approved by Cardinal Spellman before it was proposed to the membership.

At the Chicago meeting in 1967, the board authorized the formation of a committee to be called the Committee for Liaison with the Bishops' Committee on Doctrine. The members of the committee reflect the importance of this committee—the president, the ex-president, the chair of the Committee on Current Problems, and two members of the board (1967, 343). Bishop Alexander Zaleski, the chair of the newly formed Bishops' Committee on Doctrine after Vatican II, addressed the 1968 convention. He insisted that the committee was not interested in playing the role of a watchdog but that the bishops needed the help of the society in dealing with some theological and pastoral problems as they arose.

In the 1960s, the CTSA began to engage in ecumenical dialogue. Here, the influence of Vatican II was paramount, but Jaroslav Pelikan of Yale was the first non-Catholic to give a plenary address at the 1962 meeting in Pittsburgh even before the opening of Vatican II. This timing is somewhat remarkable. Only an investigation of the archives might be able to uncover the circumstances that led to this novel event. It was a very stimulating address entitled "The Protestant Concept of the Church: An Ecumenical Perspective" (1962, 131–37). Most Protestants no longer hold to an invisible church, but rather to a visible church with a visible quest for unity. In conclusion, he asked if such a unity in diversity could ever be achieved again. Not in our lifetime, and perhaps not ever. But it could happen if we all open our hearts to the transforming grace of the Holy Spirit.

Just two weeks ago we all celebrated and sang, separately and yet together:

Veni Creator Spiritus,
mentes tuorum visita.
Imple superna gratia,

Quae Tu creasti pectora.
Amen. So be it. (1962, 137)

He received a standing ovation from the members assembled there in their Roman collars. Some, and maybe even many, interpreted Pelikan's address as calling for a return to the one true Church, but the reception of the talk marked a very memorable moment in the history of the CTSA since it occurred even before Vatican II started.

The 1965 convention in Denver held the first open session in the society's history to discuss ecumenism. The two speakers were Dr. Robert McAfee Brown of Stanford and Daniel O'Hanlon of the Jesuit Theologate in California. Protestant and Catholic leaders in Denver had been invited to the session and a Q&A followed after the thirty-minute presentations (1965, 95–113). The 1966 meeting in Providence showed an increased interest in ecumenism and interreligious dialogue. An evening open session modeled on the previous event in Denver involved an address by George Lindbeck of Yale, "Karl Rahner and a Protestant View of the Sacramentality of the Ministry," followed by comments made by Maurice Duchaine (1966, 267–88). The final general session of that year's convention consisted of a Jewish-Catholic dialogue presented by Mark H. Tannenbaum, head of the Interreligious Affairs of the American Jewish Committee, and Father Edward H. Flannery who later worked on Catholic-Jewish relations for the U.S. bishops (1966, 303–22).

The CTSA invited Paul Ramsey, a Protestant ethician at Princeton University and a member and former president of the Society of Christian Ethics, as a guest observer of the 1966 convention (1966, 327). Members of the board and others often gathered after the last session of the day for a drink in the hotel suite of the board. As a courtesy, they invited Paul Ramsey, but some were not all that happy about Ramsey's presence. After a half hour or so, Ramsey was the center of attention. The members soon recognized that Ramsey was quite conservative and a good partygoer. They sat around Ramsey asking him various questions. Somewhere in the course of the evening, Ramsey blurted out, "If my fundamentalist preacher father could only see me now—a pipe in one hand, a scotch in the other, and a guest of the Catholic Theological Society of America." By this time, ecumenism was a part of the life of the CTSA.

In the later 1960s, the membership and the board also began to take stands regarding somewhat controversial issues involving the work of theologians. In April 1967, the president in the name of the board condemned the action of the board of trustees of The Catholic University of America (CUA) for not renewing my contract without any hearing or discussion and supported the unanimous decision of the faculty of the School of Theology to go on strike unless and until I was reinstated.[1] Father John L. McKenzie, SJ, who received the Spellman Award in 1967, asked the society to evaluate the charge of heresy against him made by Archbishop Robert E. Lucey based on McKenzie's book *Authority in the Church*. The officers and board concluded unanimously that the charge is unjustified and objected to some of the epithets used by the archbishop. A motion was made for the whole society to endorse this statement. Somewhat surprisingly, the vote was ninety-five in favor and thirty-five opposed, thus indicating some significant differences within the society (1968, 289).

The society in the late 1960s began working with other church groups on projects. The 1970 convention mentioned three such projects that the society became involved in. The first was a project of the CTSA working with the Urban Task Force of the U.S. Catholic Conference and the Social Theology Department of the Center for Applied Research in the Apostolate dealing with the role of the Church in society. Nine papers were prepared and sent to the twenty-seven participants as a basis for their discussions at a three-day meeting held in May in Maryland. The original papers were published as a book—*Metropolis: Christian Presence and Responsibility*.[2] The second was a project of the CTSA in conjunction with the National Federation of Priests' Councils and the journal *Chicago Studies* dealing with shared responsibility in the local church. *Chicago Studies* published the volume of papers from the project.[3] The third was a theological study on the permanent diaconate requested by the bishops' committee dealing with this subject (1970, 239). Thus, as time went on, the CTSA became involved in many other projects in addition to the annual convention.

Membership

There were 104 charter members of the society at its beginning in 1946. Eighty were religious order priests and twenty-four diocesan priests (1946, 61–65). Recall the original constitution did not explicitly mention the fact of priesthood for active membership, but associate members were priests who wanted to identify themselves with the work of the society.

The minutes of the 1947 convention show that the admissions committee rejected two applicants—a woman and a seminarian. No names were mentioned (1947, 12). The first change in membership requirements occurred in 1953. Brother Celestine Luke Salm, who had received an STD degree from Catholic University, appeared at the 1952 meeting to the consternation of some of the clerical members.[4] In 1953, he was officially admitted as an active member, and the constitutions were changed. Active membership is limited "to priests who are or have been actively engaged in the promotion of studies and research in Sacred Theology and to religious brothers who have attained the licentiate in Sacred Theology." From 1946 to 1964, 1,373 active and associate members were admitted to CTSA. In 1964, there were about 1,100 active and associate members. All were priests except for three religious brothers.[5]

Christopher Kauffman, who in 1983 launched the journal *US Catholic Historian*, strongly criticized the CTSA for its membership policies in a 1963 article in *Continuum*. Recently, he pointed out, there has been a growing number of Catholic theologians who were not priests receiving pontifical degrees and other doctorates from U.S. Catholic universities. "There is now this growing body of competent Catholic theologians who are not permitted to join the one professional society organized specifically for Catholic theologians."[6] One can only speculate about the influence of this article, but the CTSA constitutions were changed again in 1964.

The spring 1964 newsletter to the membership contained two proposed amendments regarding membership in the society. Active membership is open to all who are professionally competent. Professional competence is understood to mean the possession of at least the licentiate degree in one of the sacred sciences from a pontifical university or a doctorate in any of the sacred sciences from a nonpontifical institution of higher learning. Note here the equivalence of a pontifical licentiate with a doctorate from a nonpontifical institution. This proposed change passed without any dissent. A second proposal called for the elimination in the future of associate membership, but many in the discussion of the issue pointed out that priests for their own knowledge and development wanted to be associated with the work of the CTSA. The amendment was roundly defeated (1964, 236–37). The minutes of this meeting for the first time note the presence of book publishers who were invited by the society (1964, 227). At the 1965 convention, the nominating committee recommended two women for membership, Elizabeth Jane Farians and Cathleen M. Going, and three laymen, Albert F. Corbo, Petro B. T. Bilaniuk, and Hamilton Hess. They and all the other nominees were elected to membership without any reference being made to the new women and laymen members (1965, 162–63).

Elizabeth Farians was the first woman to attend a meeting—the 1966 Providence convention—but not without suffering a horrific experience. I had noticed a commotion as the priest secretary of the society had refused a woman entry to the banquet on Tuesday evening. I went over and talked with her, discovered her name and that she was a member of the society. I asked her to wait a moment while I called my CUA colleague Eamon Carroll, the president, and asked him to come down immediately to override the secretary. He did so, and I accompanied Elizabeth Farians into the banquet. In her book *The Second Sex*, Mary Daly tells this story in the third person, which led many people to believe that she was the person involved.

Mary Catherine Hilkert was president of the CTSA in 2005 and 2006. She invited Elizabeth Farians to the 2006 convention to honor her and commemorate the fortieth anniversary of her first attendance at a meeting. At the 2006 meeting, she was presented a plaque at the Woman's Seminar Luncheon and was a special guest of the president at the John Courtney Murray Award banquet (2006, 186). I ceremoniously accompanied her into the banquet.

In a 2005 letter to Hilkert in response to her invitation to be a guest at the 2006 convention, Farians shared some of her history. In 1958, she received a PhD in theology from St. Mary's College in Notre Dame, Indiana. She applied for membership at that time in the CTSA but was told it was only for priests. After the change in the constitution in 1964, she received a membership application and immediately responded (2016, 226).

Farians and Going both received their PhDs from the graduate program in theology at St. Mary's College in Notre Dame, Indiana. It is no digression to say a word about this pioneering endeavor. Sister Madeleva Wolff, the legendary president of St. Mary's, started the theological graduate program for women in 1943. Most students were religious women, but as time went on, more laywomen also enrolled. This was the first graduate program giving the doctorate for women in the United States and in the world. It closed after twenty-seven years because by then a number of Catholic universities started doctoral programs that also enrolled women. The St. Mary's program conferred three hundred sixty master's degrees and seventy-four doctoral degrees. Perhaps its most famous graduate was Mary Daly, the post-Christian feminist who taught for many years at Boston College.[7]

Farians and Going were not active in the life of the CTSA immediately after becoming members. Farians told me she herself never went to another meeting after 1966. The people of my generation that I talked to had never seen Going at a meeting. Farians retained her membership for a few years and Going even longer. In fact, in the late 1970s and early 1980s, Going gave papers at the conventions (e.g., 1978, 84–89; 1981, 174–77). Shortly thereafter, she became a cloistered Dominican sister but retained her membership in the CTSA (1989, 183). The first woman who most actively participated in the society was Sister Agnes Cunningham. She had been a teacher and principal in Chicago area schools before she became the first woman to receive a doctorate in theology from the Facultés Catholiques in Lyon, France. Her 1968 dissertation was on John Henry Newman and Christian humanism, but her primary interest was in patristic studies. She became a member of the CTSA in 1967 (1967, 343), a member of the board of directors in 1969 (1969, 221), and secretary of the society in 1970 (1970, 238).

Of the 613 new members from 1965 to 1971, 12.5 percent were not priests. There were thirty-eight laymen, twenty-two religious sisters, and five laywomen (1995, 302). The membership of the CTSA was beginning to change, and this change grew geometrically in the subsequent years.

The entry of African American members was much slower. The first African American member by 1960 was Joseph Nearon, a priest of the Blessed Sacrament Fathers, and fifteen years later, he was still the only one. In 1974, he admitted that Black theology had not been one of his preoccupations (1974, 413). Nevertheless, he directed the discussion of James Cone's book *Black Theology and Black Power* at the meeting in 1970 (1970, 241).

Change in Leadership

Another significant development occurred at the end of the first twenty-five-year period of the CTSA. People who were proponents of the renewal in Catholic theology associated with Vatican II took over leadership roles in the CTSA. Richard T. Doherty, who taught at St. Paul Seminary in St. Paul, Minnesota, in 1964 was the last of the 1946 charter members to serve as president. Most of the presidents before that time had been charter members with the others being long-time members. In 1969, I was elected president at age thirty-five. A person of that age should not be president of a major academic society in the United States. Presidents should have an established record as important contributors to the work of the discipline and not people who have received their doctorate only eight years before. But my presidency well illustrates the change in leadership.

Two circumstances help to explain this fact. First, Vatican II (1962–65) played a major role. All recognized that U.S. Catholic theology had no influence on Vatican II except for the exemplary work of John Courtney Murray on religious freedom. What explains this reality? There were no leading theologians in the United States who were developing any new approaches to theology in the period before Vatican II. The Church in this country was a "brick and mortar church" concentrating on the practical issues of building schools and churches to take care of the growing number of Catholics. Its primary concerns were not intellectual. For all practical purposes, CUA was the only university granting doctoral degrees in theology, and they were not all that many. Before the Second World War, CUA was almost dormant in giving theology degrees. The approach to theology in this country was primarily pastoral and not intellectual. Catholic theologians were priests who taught future priests to prepare them for their ministry. In such circumstances, theology in the United States was not making any real contribution to the theological life of the Church. European theologians were the outstanding contributors to the work of Vatican II. Most U.S. theologians who had been teaching for some time were not prepared for the changes brought about by Vatican II. As a result, many of these theologians retired from teaching soon after the council. A new generation attuned to the changes of Vatican II took over the theological task. Some of the presidents before 1970 were of the Vatican II persuasion, but they were older scholars when they became president.

Second, historical circumstances surrounding me also influenced my election as president of the CTSA. As mentioned, the president and board publicly condemned the action of the board of trustees of CUA (the membership included every archbishop in the United States, other bishops, and a comparatively few laymen; the exclusive language is accurate) in not renewing my contract without any hearing and supported the action of the CUA School of Theology in their strike. A year later in 1968, I was the spokesperson and leader for what eventually came to be over six hundred Catholic scholars in making a public statement the day after the encyclical *Humanae vitae* concluding that a

Catholic both in theory and practice can disagree with the teaching of *Humanae vitae* and still be a loyal Roman Catholic.

At the June 1968 meeting of CTSA, I was nominated for vice president, who "ordinarily" becomes president the following year. A motion from the floor, obviously attempting to avoid such a result, moved that the incumbent officers remain in office for another year. However, this motion was not accepted. I was then elected on the ballot as vice president (1968, 283). In 1969, I was the existing vice president who was nominated for president. However, another candidate was nominated from the floor, again as an attempt to keep me from holding office. On the ballot, I was elected president with a vote of ninety-nine to thirty-six (1969, 270–71).

The presidents after 1970 were all committed to the work of Vatican II, moving the society in a new direction. The opposition to my election, however, points to another important reality. The opposition in 1969 undoubtedly centered on the legitimacy of dissent from noninfallible magisterial teaching. This foreshadowed a very significant reality that developed in subsequent years. In fact, two societies later came into existence precisely to support the teaching of the papal magisterium.

THEOLOGICAL CONTENT

This section will discuss the papers that were presented at the annual conventions of the CTSA. It would be impossible to discuss all of the papers. This problem is even greater in the latter part of the first twenty-five years, when more elective papers were scheduled due to the growth of the society and the numbers attending the annual convention. My role is to select what I judge to be the most important subjects found in this time frame of twenty-five years. I have to be very conscious of my limitations and the danger of imposing my opinions and prejudices. The reader should be conscious of this inherent limitation in discussing what occurred at the meetings of the CTSA. One more objective criterion that will be used will give more importance to the presidential addresses and the papers given at plenary sessions, but that does not mean that the elective sessions will never be mentioned.

Methodological Issues

Regarding the methodological aspects of theology as found in the convention papers, the primary source for theology was the papal magisterium. There is general agreement that the Church became more centralized and the papal role grew in the latter part of the nineteenth century and the first sixty years of the twentieth century. The greater emphasis on the papal role especially affected the role of papal teaching.

From the very beginning, the *Proceedings* of the conventions also show papal teaching as the most important source of Catholic theology. Recall the paper given by Francis Connell at the very first meeting of the society on the ends of marriage, which was primarily a discussion of the papal teaching on this issue. James O'Connell in his presidential report to the third convention insisted, "It is imperative, therefore, to continue to have the approval of the *Ecclesia Docens* without which the society could not long survive" (1948, 6). President O'Connell is here using the terminology that was most prevalent at this time—the distinction between the Teaching Church (*Ecclesia Docens*) and the Learning Church (*Ecclesia Discens*). The popes and the hierarchy are the Teaching Church, and all others, including theologians, form the Learning Church. The minutes of the fourth meeting in 1949 include the letter that President Eugene Burke wrote to all the bishops when sending copies of the *Proceedings* of the conventions from the first three years. Burke told the bishops in the name of the society that "we are aware that a Society which calls itself theological necessarily depends for its norms and direction on the teaching authority of the Church" (1949, 18–19).

In 1953, John M. A. Fearns gave the first "presidential address," replacing the former report of the president, on the theological content of the teaching of Pope Pius XII. He refers to the teaching authority of the Church in the encyclical *Humani generis* as "the living voice of revelation" (1953, 180–81). In his presidential address to the twelfth annual convention in Philadelphia, George Shea summarized his talk on theology and the magisterium in this way:

> I propose to dwell on the vital intrinsic dependence of the Catholic theologian and of his science on the *Ecclesia Docens*. In other words, we are to focus our attention on the primordial truth that Sacred Theology lives and moves and has its being in the sacred magisterium....Throughout their scientific labors, theologians must take the magisterium as their norm and guide. (1957, 217)

In his presidential address to the 1959 meeting, Michael J. Murphy points out the number of times that the first thirteen volumes of the *Proceedings* refer to the teaching of Pope Pius XII. The careful reader will find in them references to sixteen of the forty encyclicals of Pius XII; to the dogmatic bull defining the dogma of the assumption; to four of the apostolic constitutions and *motu proprios*; and to about fifty of his allocutions, letters, radio addresses, and homilies. In more than 175 instances, the participants in their prepared papers have invoked the wisdom and science of the teaching of Pope Pius XII (1959, 185–92).

At the sixth annual meeting in 1951, Edmond Benard of Catholic University gave a plenary address, "The Doctrinal Value of the Ordinary Teaching of the Holy Father in View of *Humani Generis*." *Humani generis*, the 1950 encyclical of Pope Pius XII, maintained that when the pope goes out of his way to speak on a contested issue, it is no longer a matter for free debate among theologians. Theologians, however, according to Benard, are not required to stop thinking about or to stop studying it. If the theologian thinks on the basis of study some modification of the statement should be made, he should make respectful recommendations to that effect directly to the Holy See (1951, 107). Without explicitly saying so, Benard admits the teaching might need some modification, which seems to indicate in some respects it might be wrong. Benard, who was elected president at that meeting, here differs significantly from what Francis Connell said at the first meeting in 1946.

In 1967, when discussion about a change in the teaching on artificial contraception was going on, Austin Vaughan, then the vice president of the CTSA, addressed the topic of the ordinary magisterium of the universal episcopate. A theologian may withhold internal assent from such a noninfallible teaching of the universal magisterium if he finds the reasons compelling, but he cannot oppose it externally "unless circumstances indicate that the magisterium now regards it as a matter open for discussion" (1967, 16).

Two early plenary sessions well illustrate the primary importance given to the papal magisterium. In his "Theology of the Church and State" at the 1947 convention, Joseph Clifford Fenton defended the thesis that Catholics in the United States should not be so complacent about the American situation in which the state does not recognize the one true Church. To defend the need for the unity of church and state, Fenton exegetes the teachings of Popes Gregory XVI, Pius IX, and Leo XIII to prove his point (1947, 15–46). Edward Hanahoe's 1954 plenary, "The Ecumenical Movement," gives a long history of the Protestant ecumenical movement. In the end, Hanahoe appeals to many documents from the papal magisterium to condemn the approach of the ecumenical movement because Protestants must return to the one true Church founded by Jesus (1954, 140–200). Thus, throughout most of the first twenty-five years of CTSA's history, the primary source for theological truth was the teaching of the papal magisterium, which required at least external assent by theologians.

Some theological reaction to *Humanae vitae*, the 1968 encyclical of Pope Paul VI condemning artificial contraception, came to a different conclusion about the assent due to non-infallible magisterial teaching. Richard A. McCormick in his 1969 plenary address, "The Teaching Role of the Magisterium and Theologians," rejects that understanding of teaching in the Church that was generally proposed in Catholic theology before the late 1960s (1969, 239–54). Teaching itself has a different meaning and understanding in different ecclesial, historical, and cultural circumstances. The older understanding of teaching in the Church unduly separated the *Docens* from the *Discens* function by identifying the teaching role with a single group in the Church (the hierarchy) and insisting on just the judicial aspect of teaching. There are different ecclesial, historical, and cultural factors that have influenced the understanding of teaching in the postconciliar Church. The teaching dimension of the Church is a pluridimensional process. In this process, the magisterium or teaching function involves three interrelated components—the prophetic charism, the pastoral-doctrinal component of the hierarchy, and the scientific charism of the theologian. To carry out its authoritative and authentic teaching role properly, the hierarchical magisterium must listen to the prophetic and theological charisms in the Church. The hierarchical magisterium needs to listen and learn before it can truly teach authentically. *Humanae vitae* and the reaction to it have shown the problems in the present reality. The hierarchical office will be truly authentic in its teaching only if it understands its role in listening to the prophetic and theological charisms that are part of the total teaching role in the Church.

McCormick's paper does two things. First, it explains why theological dissent from noninfallible magisterial teaching is a possibility. Second, it does not make the case primarily by citing papal documents. The CTSA in the first twenty-five years of its existence thus mirrors what occurred with regard to the hierarchical teaching office in the Church. It is no longer the primary source of theological knowledge, and the proper response to it at times can be dissent. In a more positive way, it points to the need of the three components of the teaching role of the Church to work together for the sake of the search for truth.

A second source for theological and philosophical knowledge that changed in the course of the first twenty-five years of the CTSA is Thomistic philosophy and theology as *the* Catholic approach. In 1879, Pope Leo XIII in his encyclical *Aeterni patris* called for the restoration of Catholic philosophy and theology according to the mind and method of Thomas Aquinas. Subsequent popes and the 1917 Code of Canon Law reinforced the centrality of Thomistic philosophy and theology in Catholic thought.[8] Recall that at the first convention in 1946, William O'Connor insisted that Catholic theology is Thomistic. E. Ferrer Smith ends his presidential address in 1963 after the first session of Vatican II by insisting that St. Thomas's teaching is the guide, the guardian, and fruitful source of a new era of theology. This conclusion, he maintains, is not derived from past encomiums showered on Thomas's thought over the centuries. The relevance and centrality of the teaching of Aquinas have come from personal, intimate, close study and conversation with the mind of St. Thomas. In his profundity we can find a universal vitality capable of dealing with the issues of the times (1963, 196).

Gerard A. Vanderhaar, then a Dominican priest as was Ferrer Smith, began his 1966 paper, "The Status of Scholastic Philosophy in Theology," with the observation that until recently it was assumed by all both inside and outside the Church that Catholic teaching was a firm structure built on the foundations of Scholastic philosophy. The events of the previous five years, especially Vatican II, forced a reappraisal of that de facto situation. The theology emerging from the council is not at all clearly Thomistic; the language of the documents of Vatican II is not Scholastic; the categories of Scholastic thought are conspicuously absent (1966, 71). For Vanderhaar, Scholasticism is outmoded; Thomism is inadequate. Theology today must be scriptural, evolutionary, and pastoral. But even here, we can profit from the genuine contributions of Thomism without being bound by all its restrictions. Thomism is breathtaking and inspiring and spoke eloquently of God and humankind to a past age (1966, 92–93).

Thomistic natural law was an important source and the method for Catholic moral theology before Vatican II. In the mid-1960s, much discussion in the theological literature focused on artificial contraception and involved the two issues of the proper response to the teaching of the papal magisterium and the natural law that was proposed as the basis for this teaching. Examples of such approaches in CTSA presentations begin with Connell's talk on the ends of marriage at the first convention in 1946 and later included topics of rhythm, overpopulation, and newer issues as they came along, such as the so-called birth control pill.

Three papers in the CTSA conventions in the mid-1960s deal with natural law in light of the discussion over contraception. They take very different approaches but help to illuminate the understanding of natural law and its role in Catholic philosophy and theology at that time. In 1965, Robert Johann, a Jesuit philosopher at the seminary at Shrub Oak, New York, delivered his paper "Responsible Parenthood: A Philosophical View," which was the first paper at the CTSA that disagreed with the Catholic teaching on contraception. His paper was a philosophical hypothesis that totally prescinds from the Church's teaching, which is a theological issue (1965, 157). On the basis of his ethics of responsibility, he argues philosophically for the need for contraception for spouses. He even claims that his approach is a natural law approach, but one that looks at the human being as a personal nature open to the absolute and not simply a determinate structure alongside others, which results in absolutizing the physical structures of the marital act (1965, 124). Johann thus claims his approach is based on natural law, but it is not the Thomistic theory of natural law proposed by the papal magisterium.

In 1963, Gerald Kelly of the Jesuit theologate in Kansas presented his paper "Contraception and Natural Law," discussing the natural law precisely in light of its use condemning artificial contraception. We Catholic theologians already know from Church authority that contraception is wrong. Why, then, should we discuss what reason has to say about it? There are three objectives or purposes for Catholic theologians in proposing the natural law reasonings against artificial contraception. First, arguments based on reason give us a more profound insight into why contraception is immoral. Second, the arguments from reason show both Catholics and others that our teachings are reasonable. Some add a third objective—to convince unbelievers on the basis of reason alone that contraception is absolutely immoral. Kelly believes, however, the moral impossibility of an adequate knowledge of the natural law is so profound and widespread that with some rare exceptions, only those accept this truth who are aided by some kind of religious conviction (1963, 27–28). Kelly's final point goes against the general Catholic understanding of the time that natural law can and should be convincing to all people of goodwill.

In the same mid-1960s time frame, Paul McKeever, who was then the vice president of the CTSA in 1967, addressed the issue of theology and natural law. McKeever begins in a somewhat defensive way. Even with the approach of Vatican II, the modern scriptural revival, and the pertinence of contemporary philosophical insights, natural law remains. By natural law, he means the concept given best expression by Thomas Aquinas. Yes, natural law *theoria* arose in the particular circumstances of the Middle Ages, and today we recognize the reality of historical consciousness. But the magisterium of the Church has canonized natural law *theoria* in general and has insisted on its existence and knowability through reason and revelation and its direct pertinence to specifically Christian morality. McKeever concludes from the theological point of view that natural law must be considered a permanent and enduring part of Christian moral doctrine (1967, 223–36).

Thus, these three papers from the CTSA meetings in the mid-1960s indicate the extensive discussion about natural law at the time, often in relationship to contraception. Subsequent discussions appealing to Vatican II and the objections against *Humanae vitae* by revisionist Catholic moral theologians have strongly disagreed with the understanding of natural law proposed by the papal magisterium, especially in the area of sexuality. But the papal magisterium and some theologians continue to support the natural law theory found in *Humanae vitae*.

The textbooks of theology in the time frame up to Vatican II were called the manuals. The primary disciplines in Catholic seminaries and theologates were dogmatic theology, dealing with beliefs and doctrines, and moral theology, dealing with life and actions. The manuals of dogmatic theology followed the method of stating a thesis and proving it. As indicated earlier, the thesis was stated, the terms were explained, the adversaries were discussed, and the thesis was proved by the teaching of the Church with the attached theological note (i.e., how such a topic is related to the different levels of Church teaching), the teaching of Scripture and tradition, and often followed by various scholions. John Courtney Murray in his 1956 convention paper points out the problems with the thesis approach. The sources are studied after the thesis has been stated. The danger is that one finds proof for the thesis in the sources, but the correct method transposes the order. The study of the sources should come first because the sources give rise to true theological inquiry. The method of theology should be a method of inquiry based on the reading of the sources (1956, 224). For these reasons, the manuals of dogmatic theology ceased to exist after the theologians absorbed the work of Vatican II.

Murray also sees in the thesis method the danger of formalism. The living processes of theological inquiry and understanding are crippled or killed within the categories of the thesis method (1956, 223). In my own words, based on my experience as a theological student in Rome in the second half of the 1950s, the thesis method too often reduced the study of theology just to memory. Looking back from a Vatican II and post–Vatican II perspective, one can see in Murray's position a return to the sources, which with the need for aggiornamento was the driving force of the work for the renewal of theology at Vatican II. Murray's problems with the thesis approach as not giving enough primacy to the sources also comes from his own experience. In 1956, he had finished his six historical treatises in *Theological Studies* dealing with the sources touching on the role of church and state. As a result of these studies, he concluded that religious freedom in light of the changed circumstances of the twentieth century should now be accepted by the Church.[9]

The manuals of moral theology before Vatican II had their own distinctive format with the purpose of knowing what acts are sinful and the degrees of sinfulness. Their purpose was to train future confessors as judges in the sacrament of penance. James W. O'Brien's paper at the fourth meeting of the CTSA in 1949, "The Scientific Teaching of Moral Theology," strongly criticizes these manuals and the method they employ. The science of these manuals is the science of sin. It is conceivable that a seminarian could learn what the manuals say about moral theology without being a theologian at all. The moral theology manuals treat only the bad acts and not the good. Moral theology at that time had lost its character, both as a science and as a theology (1949, 193–94).

In this quite short paper, O'Brien sees the solution as the return to the teaching and method of Thomas Aquinas. In these few pages, he does not develop the precise details of this approach but insists that such an approach would bring together not only what acts are bad but also what acts are good, thus bringing ascetical theology into the realm of moral theology (1949, 194–95).

O'Brien's criticism of the manuals of moral theology had no real effect on the teaching of moral theology in this country. Nevertheless, he implicitly pointed out a paradoxical situation—most Catholic moral theologians at the time would probably have said they were Thomistic, but in reality they were not. The manuals of moral theology were deeply entrenched in the Catholic ethos at the time, and they were not going to change until Vatican II. The renewal of moral theology beginning just before and after Vatican II gave primary importance to the scriptural basis and not the Thomistic basis of the discipline.

Two papers from the CTSA conventions in this time frame criticized the approach of the manuals dealing with ecclesiology (*De Ecclesia*). Recall that at the very first meeting in 1946, Joseph Bluett's paper "The Theological Significance of the Encyclical *Mystici Corporis*" called for a new approach to the understanding of the Church and not the approach found in the manuals of ecclesiology. The manuals reflected the older circumstances (e.g., the Reformation denial of a visible Church) calling for an understanding of the Church as visible, the kingdom of God on earth that carries on the message of Jesus. The tract on the Church was called fundamental theology because it served as the basis for all the other aspects of dogmatic theology. But *Mystici Corporis*, the 1943 encyclical of Pope Pius XII, calls for a different approach. The Church is the Mystical Body of Christ because it is replete with indwelling divinity and is formed and vitalized from within by that divinity. The indwelling divine Spirit penetrates every aspect of the Church and every part of its supernatural life and unity (1946, 52–60).

Richard Redmond's paper, "How Should *De Ecclesia* Be Treated in Scientific Theology," at the seventeenth convention in 1962 makes a similar proposal. The manuals of *De Ecclesia*, especially in response to the Reformation, stressed the visibility or external aspects of the Church. Based on the four marks of the Church (one, holy, catholic, and apostolic), one could prove that the Catholic Church is the true Church of Jesus (1962, 144–45). Vatican I, with its emphasis on the Church's authority, stressed the visibility of the Church with its papal and hierarchical structure. The existing manuals of *De Ecclesia* have this apologetic and not dogmatic purpose. They want to show that the Church exists and is God's authentic spokesperson on earth. In the light of *Mystici Corporis* and subsequent theological developments, there is need for a truly dogmatic treatise on the Church with emphasis on the spiritual reality of the Church as the Mystical Body of Christ carrying on the work of redemption (1962, 153–60).

A later criticism of the dogmatic manuals comes in Edwin Kaiser's 1959 address, "The Theology of the Resurrection of Christ" (1959, 28–53). The manuals discuss the resurrection primarily from the apologetic perspective. The fact of the resurrection proves that Jesus is divine and we can trust all that he has said and done. The resurrection was not primarily treated from the viewpoint of its relationship to salvation. One important reason here that Kaiser does not develop is Anselm's theory of redemption as found primarily in the cross and death of Jesus. The death of Jesus is required in justice because only the divine person can atone for the infinite offense of human sin against God. The salvific meaning is attached to the death of Jesus but not to the resurrection. Kaiser's paper relies on contemporary European theologians such as Francis X. Durwell, Karl Rahner, and Joseph Schmitt. He also develops the teaching on the resurrection in Paul's letters and touches on the teaching from the patristic period through the Middle Ages.

The resurrection is a mystery of faith and an integral part of redemption. Easter is the paschal feast that celebrates the resurrection. Through baptism and the other sacraments, we share in the life of the risen Lord. Kaiser refers to the paschal mystery that has become a central term after Vatican II. He also brings out the eschatological dimension of the resurrection. The resurrection of Christ is the cause of our sharing in the newness of life through grace and the fullness of life in eternity.

Some papers given at the CTSA thus show some new approaches disagreeing with what is found in the manuals of dogmatic theology. Such a reality indicates that there were some calls for change even before Vatican II. In fact, we need to remember there would never have been a Vatican II without the changes that were springing up before Vatican II in the areas of theology, liturgy, and ecumenism. But the strength of these developments was found in Europe, as well illustrated in Kaiser's 1959 article on the resurrection, and not in the United States. Except in the area of religious liberty, U.S. theology made no significant contribution to the theology of Vatican II.

One source of theology as part of its method that is not highlighted in the CTSA *Proceedings* in the first twenty-five years is the role of Scripture in theology. In light of Vatican II, theologians today would see Scripture as the primary source of theology. One paper by Eugene Burke at the 1959 meeting does address "Scripture as *Locus Theologicus*" (1959, 54–96). The author insists there are two different types of theology: speculative theology and scriptural theology. The real methodological question is what role Scripture plays in speculative theology, but Burke is not primarily concerned with this issue. He insists on the two different types of theology and often refers to Scripture as exegesis. In passing, the article rejects using Scripture as a proof text. The final section discusses speculative theology and exegesis but develops the point that all fruitful exegesis supposes a philosophical framework and so, ultimately, a theology. The popes from Leo XIII on have insisted on a full and sound theological formation to ensure a sound Catholic exegesis. Notice that Burke sees speculative theology as giving primary importance to dogma and Church teaching, which explains why it is also called dogmatic theology.

In 1955, the Scripture scholar Roderick A. F. McKenzie's paper, "The Concept of Biblical Theology," also stresses the difference between biblical theology and speculative theology (1955, 48–66). Biblical theology treats the doctrine of God contained in the Scripture analyzed and systematized in biblical terms. It is distinguished from speculative theology, which uses philosophy as a scaffolding for its construction. In his conclusion, however, he points out that when the infant biblical theology has advanced toward its perfection, it will offer to speculative theology an immense accretion of materials on which speculative theology can build.

One notes with interest that in this time frame, biblical scholars gave about ten papers at the conventions of the CTSA. As time went on, Roderick A. F. McKenzie's recognition that biblical scholarship could provide materials for speculative theology was born out, for example, by two papers presented by the scripture scholar

Bruce Vawter. Vawter shows Scripture has much to contribute to speculative theology. In his 1959 paper on "Messianic Prophecies in Apologetics," Vawter argues against the older apologetic approach found in the manuals that one can prove on the basis of the Old Testament that Jesus was the Messiah who was prophesied. On the contrary, it was the resurrection that proved to the apostles that Jesus was the promised Messiah and Redeemer, and only in the light of this knowledge did they see the fulfillment of prophecy (1959, 97–119). In his 1967 paper, "The Biblical Theology of Divorce," Vawter concludes that Jesus's command regarding divorce is not a promulgation of divine law but a word addressed to the Christian conscience informed by divine grace. Earlier in the article, he points out that the exception clause in Matthew 5:32 indicates that the early Church did make exceptions in the more absolute words of Jesus (1967, 223–43).

In Catholic theology outside the conventions of the CTSA, there was some strong friction between theologians and biblical scholars who were using the historical-critical method.[10] There is one indication of this in the convention papers themselves. In 1965, Raymond Brown gave an elective seminar paper on "The Biblical Evidence for the Human Knowledge of Christ" (1965, 159). In his talk on the basis of his historical-critical method, he contended that Jesus did not know from the beginning that he was the Messiah. The story went around that Brown did not want his paper published, because he had been under severe attack from some in the Church, including theologians because of his biblical positions.[11] This experience thus shows that implicitly there was some indication in the CTSA conventions of this tension.

A good illustration of how Scripture should play a fundamental role in theology is illustrated in Bernard Häring's 1963 paper, "Christian Morality as a Mirror Image of the Mystery of the Church." Häring's paper exemplifies what Vatican II later called for—the fundamental and basic importance of Scripture

43

as a source for theology (1963, 3–24). (Häring was the first European to address the CTSA [1995, 295].) Häring's paper was the first to recognize the primary role of Scripture in theology.

This section has studied the primary methodological issues discussed in the first twenty-five years of the CTSA. One sees here the significant developments between the pre–Vatican II period and the post–Vatican II times.

Theological Issues

This section will discuss the issues treated in the first quarter century in the meetings of the CTSA. It is practically impossible to discuss all the subjects developed in this time frame. At best, one could barely just mention these issues. I will discuss in some detail four issues: (1) the beginnings of the discussion in U.S. theology of the church-state issue, which later became the major contribution of the U.S. Church to Vatican II; (2) Mariology, which was the most treated issue with three articles in the first four years of the society and which reflected the life and theology of the U.S. Church at the time; (3) the failure to relate in any depth to the race issue, which was so important to the life of the country from the 1950s on; (4) an early (1969) paper on the role of women in the Church, an issue that would become very important in subsequent years.

The most significant content issue discussed in the first twenty-five years of the CTSA was the issue related to church-state relations. The earlier methodological section analyzed the different methodologies developed by Joseph Clifford Fenton and John Courtney Murray in discussing this issue. Fenton relied primarily on papal documents, whereas Murray insisted on a historical approach. Fenton basically supported the thesis that a Catholic government should repress heresy. Murray, in the 1948 article, denies that the government has an obligation to repress heresy, which was a part of the larger question of church-state, which he developed later.

Murray began his 1948 paper describing the position then taken in the United States on the church-state issue. The ideal order, or thesis, proposed the union of church and state. However, in hypothesis or in the practical order, the Church could tolerate the separation of church and state because ours is not a Catholic state. Murray in the 1948 article is dealing just with this narrower issue of the Catholic government's repression of heresy. His whole approach is based on the importance of historical realities and historical development. This emphasis on changing historical facts serves as the basis for his approach. For Murray, there is no distinction between thesis (the ideal) and hypothesis (the existing order). There is no ideal. Different types of states have existed over time, and none of them can be said to be the ideal — the monarchical, patriarchal, dictatorial, democratic, and so on.

In this early 1948 article, Murray recognizes the important differences among society, the state, and government. Society includes much more than the state. The Catholic position affirming the union of church and state and the government's obligation to repress heresy is based on the recognition that the state is a creature of God and has a natural law obligation to worship God in the way that God wants to be worshiped.

In the 1948 article, Murray insists that the state aids the Church only through the exercise of its own native power, which is human in its origin, temporal in its finality, and limited in its competence. The civil power is limited and is not to be considered an auxiliary function of the Church to be used for the Church's own ends. Murray here affirms both the autonomy and the limited competency of the state. The state is no longer the subject of an obligation to worship God in the way that God wants to be worshiped. Just as the state has no power to define the Church, so it has no power to impose the definition of the Church as accepted from its citizens on those of its citizens who do not freely by their own personal act of faith embrace the Church.

In this long article, Murray reviews the different theories of church-and-state relationship, beginning with the direct power of the church over the temporal power of the state; Robert Bellermine's theory of indirect power of the church over the state, that is really a direct power limited to exceptional use; and finally John of Paris's indirect power, which insists that the spiritual does not directly touch the temporal power. In his subsequent essays in *Theological Studies* in the 1950s, Murray continued to deepen his historical analysis to come to the conclusion of the need for religious freedom.

Francis Connell responded to Murray's paper and disagreed with his position based on the doctrine of the kingship of Christ (1948, 98–101). Fenton, Connell, and others in the subsequent years continued to disagree with Murray as he developed his teaching on the separation of church and state.

From 1947 to 1949, there were three papers dealing with Mariology. In 1947, a plenary paper by Edward J. Wuenschel addressed "The Definability of the Assumption." Pius XII, in a 1946 encyclical, said he had received many requests for a solemn definition of the assumption of Mary, and he was now consulting the bishops of the world about the definability of this teaching. Wuenschel sees this as the last step before the definition. The article develops the reasons supporting the definition that the doctrine of the assumption is contained in the deposit of faith entrusted to the Church through the apostles (1947, 72–102).

At the 1948 meeting, Clement Fuerst led a discussion on "Mary Co-Redemptrix and Mediatrix of All Graces" (1948, 126–27). Fuerst's short two-page paper presents the status of the questions. Some claim the title only in the broad sense, and others maintain that Mary is co-redemptrix in the strict sense based on her immediate moral cooperation in the redemptive acts of Christ.

Kilian J. Healy's 1949 paper, "The Theology of the Doctrine of the Immaculate Heart of Mary" (1949, 102–27), first traces the developments through three stages—the period of preparation from the beginning through the twelfth century; the period of private cult; and the period from the seventeenth century on, the growing public and liturgical cult of this devotion and teaching. A longer section explains the doctrinal basis of this cult. He concludes that just as Jesus came into the world through the heart of Mary, so through the heart of Mary the world must go to Jesus.

Gerard Owens's paper at the 1954 convention, "Historical Development of the Dogma of the Immaculate Conception: Obstacles Inhibiting Understanding and Acceptance" (1954, 67–101), develops by showing how the acceptance of the dogma overcame three difficulties.

Mariology was a contentious issue at Vatican II. A strong minority wanted a separate document on Mary, and some insisted she be given the title Co-Redemptrix and Mediatrix of All Graces—the two titles discussed at the 1948 meeting of the CTSA. But the majority did not accept these ideas. Instead of a separate document, Mary was included as the eighth chapter in the document on the Church. Mary's role was within the Church.[12]

In his presidential address to the 1966 meeting, Eamon Carroll of Catholic University built on this approach. Chapter 7 of the Vatican II document deals with the eschatological nature of the Church and its union with the Church in heaven, which is known as the Communion of Saints. His address deals with the role of Mary in the Communion of Saints. He dialogues with early Protestant reactions to this connection of Mary to the Communion of Saints. This issue is a challenge for all the Christian churches. In the process, Carroll recognizes exaggerations in Catholic practice in the past and urges Protestants to delve more deeply into the relationship with Mary to the Communion of Saints. In the light of the contemporary Catholic recognition of the role of the Spirit in other Christian churches and the need for a truly historical theology, Catholic theologians are challenged to examine a wide range of important questions related to the role of Mary in the Communion of Saints (1966, 249–65). Thus, for Carroll, it seems that Mariology is no longer a divisive issue between Catholics and Protestants, but a place where true dialogue should take place, even though differences continue to exist. Such a dialogue did not play a role in earlier Catholic approaches at the meetings of the CTSA.

As mentioned, it is impossible to examine all the issues discussed in the papers at the CTSA convention. A critical reading, however, also strives to uncover important issues that were not discussed or did not receive any in-depth treatment. In my judgment, the primary example here is the failure to deal with the reality of racism that was so prevalent in this country in the 1950s and especially the 1960s. There were only two papers dealing with aspects of the question when the enormity of the issue called for a much greater response by Catholic theologians.

In 1958, Francis J. Gilligan's paper, "Moral Aspects of Segregation in Education," dealt with this issue especially in light of the 1954 Supreme Court decision in *Brown v. Board of Education* that declared involuntary segregation of schools was unconstitutional, thus rejecting the "separate but equal" justification that had supported such segregation earlier. Catholics earlier might have justified such segregation by saying it was necessary for public welfare and peace, but there is also an important ethical proviso to this principle — provided other more basic human rights are not violated. Involuntary segregation is and was morally wrong because it violates the basic human rights of Blacks. Now that the Supreme Court has acted, Catholics cannot say the law is unjust for the very same reason that involuntary segregation involves the denial of basic rights of Black people. Gilligan points out that the basic problem in race relations in the United States is the prejudice of white persons. In the light of the Last Judgment, it will most probably be revealed that almost every white person in the South and in the North has been affected to some extent with the sinful virus of race prejudice and must struggle to overcome this prejudice (1958, 51–60). With regard to Gilligan, he was the first Catholic theologian in the United States to write a monograph on race relations—*The Morality of the Color Line: An Examination of the Right and Wrong of the Discriminations against the Negro in the United States.* This was originally a doctoral dissertation written under the direction of John A. Ryan at the Catholic University of America in 1928.[13]

Joseph Leonard's 1964 paper, "Current Theological Questions in Race Relations," accepts the general principle that racial discrimination is immoral and then briefly discusses five related issues (1964, 81–91). Leonard belonged to the Josephite order, whose mission was to the Black community. Leonard points out that both the magisterium and theologians were very late in realizing the immorality of compulsory segregation. His explanation of this fact seems to be rather weak and timid. Now we have come in the light of personalistic values and other contemporary factors to appreciate the problem in the same way that occurred in other issues, such as interest on loans or the right of adult children to choose their own spouses. He never raises the question of the culpability involved in not recognizing the enormity of the problem of racial prejudice and discrimination. In the short treatment of the morality of demonstrations, he admits the need to consider a multitude of factors in dealing with the morality of peaceful demonstrations, such as those of Martin Luther King Jr. As King pointed out, these demonstrations are peaceful, but there is the danger of occasioning riots and other serious damage to persons and property. Such demonstrations have also had a very positive effect, however, on the self-respect of Blacks. Thus, there are many factors that must be taken account of in making prudential judgments, but all have to agree that the present situation of segregation is wrong.[14]

Leonard's treatment is necessarily short, but one has a feeling that it is primarily a casuistic approach to what individuals should do. The social morality of segregation and prejudice, however, deserve much greater attention. The failure of the CTSA to address the social situation in other papers involves a continuing failure to recognize the social sin of segregation and prejudice that had become so much more prevalent as the 1950s and 1960s progressed.

Considering future events, one important plenary session at the 1969 meeting stands out. Agnes Cunningham addressed the topic "The Ministry of Woman in the Church" (1969, 124–41). As mentioned earlier, she was the first woman to be an active member of the society as well as, in this instance, the first woman to give a plenary address. This was an important, fascinating, and somewhat puzzling paper. In the beginning, she clearly states what she will do — to suggest that the ordination of women to the ministerial priesthood in the Roman Catholic Church is a principle to be affirmed and is consonant with the mission of the Church in her spatial, temporal reality. In this particular historical moment, it might well be a guarantee as well as an expression of the orthodoxy of faith in the Christian community. She maintains that the evidence of the past as well as the present points to the fact that woman has been deprived of her rightful role and function in Christianity.

Her principal argument is anthropological — the concept of woman, which is a question of anthropology — an authentically Christian vision of "man." Note here at this time the use of exclusive language, which was the *lingua franca* of the day. Her position avoids the extremes of antifeminism and a feministic plea for the liberation of woman. Perhaps here she was very conscious of the overwhelmingly male audience of priests she addressed. The paper affirms the concept of woman as *homo*—one who shares the nature and destiny of humankind. Man and woman are creatures of the one absolute. Theology must encompass the mystery of duality and di-unity, which is expressed in differentiation and totalization of mankind. The equality of the sexes is not based on an identity of role or of function. Woman is the helper who stands with man. Neither man nor woman is an absolute, totally independent being. Man and woman discover in each other an equality of complementarity in trying to live out what humans are called to do in the cosmos. Note here the use of complementarity to support basic equality—the mystery of di-unity. Later feminists strongly objected to complementarity because in practice it always meant subordination. Cunningham maintains that in Jesus Christ we find extreme duality and extreme unity. The differentiation of persons by gender is not dominated by monistic discrimination. Christ assumed all humanity so that all might be transformed. Unity is possible only because of duality. The proper approach to the incarnation and eschatology insists on history as evolutionary and progressive. One cannot appeal to evidences of the past to resist the authentic evolution of human progress.

In the light of the preceding, one is not prepared for the short three conclusions—to affirm woman's accession to ministerial priesthood, to initiate authentic theological discussion on this principle, and in preparation for the moment when ordination of woman to priesthood will be a reality, to establish an order of deaconesses. Perhaps she is satisfied with just proposing her vision and principle while practically accepting the present reality in the Church. But this paper remains very significant in making the argument for the ordination of women in the Catholic Church.

No attempt has been made to consider all the issues discussed in this twenty-five-year time frame. The four issues mentioned here stand out because of their significance both within and beyond this time frame. John Courtney Murray's 1948 article concentrated on one part of the religious freedom issue, which in light of Murray's later development became the most important U.S. contribution to the work of Vatican II. The great emphasis on Mariology and the early attempts to see Mary in relationship with redemption and grace were replaced by Vatican II's seeing Mary as part of the document on the Church. The two papers dealing with race indicate the failure of CTSA and Catholic theology in general in even recognizing the enormity of the race problem in this country. On the other hand, the 1969 article supporting women's ordination to priesthood foreshadowed the many subsequent attempts to change the teaching and position of the Church, which nevertheless has continued all these years.

Chapter 3

THE CATHOLIC THEOLOGICAL SOCIETY OF AMERICA, 1971–1995

This chapter, like the previous one, will consider first the internal life of the society and then the theology of the papers delivered at the annual meetings.

THE INTERNAL LIFE OF THE SOCIETY

The internal life of the society will focus on three subjects — the members and the meetings, the research projects, and the tensions experienced between theologians and the hierarchical magisterium.

Members and Meetings

The membership requirements were changed in 1970 and 1974. Active membership requires the doctorate in theological or related studies, but the admissions committee can make exceptions. Associate membership requires the licentiate in one of the sacred sciences or significantly advanced participation in a doctoral program in these areas (Wister, 1995, 303). As a result, associate membership now can become a step toward full membership.

There are many areas of growth that occurred in this twenty-five-year period. The total members, active and associate, was 1,150 in 1977 and 1,471 in 1992. The number of female members increased dramatically from 52 active and 10 associate members in 1977 to 221 active and 35 associate members in 1992. The growth is due to a number of factors. First, in this time frame, many Catholic universities were granting doctoral degrees in theology. These programs were geared to providing more professors to teach in colleges and universities. Recall the fact that before 1960, the theology courses in Catholic colleges were not academically respectable, most often taught by priests or religious who did not have doctoral degrees and tended to be catechetical in nature. Vatican II also strongly influenced people to be interested in Catholic theology. In this context, it should be noted that Brother Luke Salm, who was the first nonpriest member in 1953, in 1975 became the first nonpriest to serve as president of the CTSA (Wister, 1995, 295, 298).

In the same time frame, more women gave papers at the convention and were elected to the board of directors and other positions. In 1975, Sarah Butler, as part of the "Challenge to Theology" section, gave a paper on "The Situation of Women in Society." Here she addressed the massive task facing all Americans to liberate women from oppression and bring about true equality. She concluded her paper by urging that women and men theologians call on the Church leaders to witness to the order of redemption and end official sexism in the Church by removing the sexual barrier to ordination (1975, 203–20).

Some women began to talk about the feasibility of women members gathering at a special time that would not be in competition with any other sessions. Catherine LaCugna and Elizabeth Johnson proposed such a session, which was readily accepted by the board. The first women's breakfast took place on Friday morning at the 1987 meeting in Philadelphia. This breakfast continued in 1988 and 1989. After some discussion, it was decided that, instead of a breakfast meeting, there would be a luncheon on the Saturday at noon after the regular convention ended, followed by a women's seminar open to all interested CTSA members. Such a luncheon and seminar took place at the 1990 meeting in San Francisco. The Women's Seminar in Constructive Theology met on Saturday afternoon after the close of the regular meeting for the next four years (Johnson and Patrick, 2006, 320–26). In 1994, the venue for the women's seminar was changed again because the convention now ended on Sunday at noon and not Saturday. The seminar was held on Thursday afternoon before the opening session of the convention on Thursday evening. In 1995, Anne O'Hara Graf assumed the leadership role with the seminar. To this day, the seminar continues to take place on Thursday afternoons (Johnson and Patrick, 2006, 320–26).

Agnes Cunningham in 1978 was the first woman president of CTSA. Monika Hellwig was president in 1987, Anne Patrick in 1990, and Lisa Cahill in 1993. Early John Courtney Murray Award winners were Monika Hellwig in 1984 and Margaret Farley in 1992, and in 1995, John T. and Denise Carmody became the first married couple to win the John Courtney Murray Award. This was the first time since 1947 that more than one person had received what was then the Cardinal Spellman Award. Thus, by the fiftieth anniversary of the CTSA, women theologians were a vital part of the society.

Joseph Nearon was the only African American member of the CTSA before 1970. Preston Williams of Harvard gave a plenary address titled "Religious and Social Aspects of Roman Catholic and Black American Relationships" at the 1973 meeting. At the 1974 meeting with Richard McBrien as president, Joseph Nearon made a preliminary report, or as he called it a pre-preliminary report, on the Research Committee for Black Theology (1974, 413–70). In a longer paper at the 1975 convention, Nearon pointed out that the Catholic Church in this country needs to bring about a competent group of Black Catholic theologians (1975, 177–202). It would be a long time before there would be such a number of Black Catholic theologians. The 1975 convention is noteworthy because it had papers not only on Black theology but also on women and Catholic Hispanics in this country.

The first baby steps toward a group of competent Black Catholic theologians came from Black Catholic women theologians. Beginning in the early 1980s, Jamie Phelps played a significant role. In a panel on "Women and Power in the Church," Phelps provided a Black Catholic perspective. She recognized the role played by a number of Black Catholic organizations in the 1970s on the need to combat racism within the Church and emphasized that the Church will not be firmly rooted in the Black community until that community has Black ministers of salvation (1982, 119–23). In a plenary session panel in 1989, Phelps addressed the topic of "Providence and Histories: African American Perspectives with the Emphasis on the Perspective of Black Liberation Theology" (1989, 12–18). At the 1990 convention, Phelps was elected to the board of directors, the first Black woman to play such a role (1990, 144). In 1990, Diana Hayes, a Black Catholic laywoman, moderated the breakout session on "African-Americans and Inculturation" (1990, 80–82). In 1991, Shawn Copeland addressed the convention theme of "Theology as Intellectually Vital Inquiry" from the perspective of Black theology in a workshop moderated by Jamie Phelps (1991, 49–57). Thanks to these pioneering Black women theologians, Black theology began to have a role, although it was a small role, in the CTSA.

Virgilio P. Elizondo played a major role in the CTSA, and in the Catholic theological community in general, in developing a Latino theology. In a workshop session, he spoke on "A Challenge to Theology: The Situation of Hispanic Americans." He pithily described his people as twice conquered, twice colonized, and twice oppressed (1975, 163–76). In 1981, in a workshop on Aspects of the Local Church, he read a paper, "The Hispanic Church in the USA: A Local Ecclesiology." He did not advocate a separate church but instead challenged the Church in the United States for a truly more Catholic expression of the Church (1981, 155–70). In 1993, Elizondo presented a plenary paper, "Hispanic Theology and Popular Piety: From Interreligious Encounter to a New Ecumenism." His thesis was that just as we need a new interrelatedness within the communion of Christian churches, so we need a new interrelatedness within the communion of world religions (1993, 1–14).

In addition to Elizondo, Orlando Espín, Sixto Garcia, and Roberto Goizueta addressed the issues of Hispanic life and theology. In 1987, Orlando Espín and Sixto Garcia discussed "Hispanic American Theology" (1987, 114–19) and, in 1988, "The Sources of Hispanic Theology" (1988, 122–25). Espín and Garcia's 1989 paper "Lilies of the Field: An Hispanic Theology of Providence and Human Responsibility" criticizes the consumerism, profit-imposed values, racism, and other forms of discrimination in American society, and also challenges the mainstream theologies of providence (1989, 70–90). Espín was elected to the board of directors in 1991 (1991, 209).

At the 1992 meeting, Jamie Phelps reported to the board that there are very few African Americans with doctorates in theology. Two women religious and two laywomen had doctorates. At the same meeting, board member Orlando Espín reported there were fifty to sixty Hispanic theologians, but the CTSA was perceived as not really interested in them and their concerns. The board decided to appoint a committee to develop and circulate an instrument among members of the CTSA to identify African

Americans and other underrepresented ethnic/racial Catholic graduate and doctoral students and faculty in the field of theology and related disciplines within their institutions as a first step toward recruitment (1992, 189). In 1993, the committee dealing with underrepresented groups was constituted. This committee had done some preliminary work and was preparing a grant proposal. The board would consider sponsoring the grant proposal when it was submitted (1993, 185–86). However, there is no mention of the committee and its work in the minutes of the following two conventions.

Throughout the period from 1971 to 1995, the CTSA continued to grow in its membership and in groups that had been unrepresented in the first twenty-five years of its existence. There was, however, one group whose numbers, at least percentagewise, were drastically diminished — seminary professors. At the very beginning, the CTSA was exclusively a society of priest seminary professors. According to the statistics provided by Robert Wister, only 19 percent of the membership in 1992 were associated with seminaries and theological unions (1995, 304). Unions such as the Chicago Theological Union were formed by a group of religious orders to educate their students for the priesthood.

Personal observation and experience indicate an important aspect not found in Wister's statistics. By 1995, there was a great falling off of membership from diocesan seminaries. In the early days, diocesan seminaries such as those of New York, Newark, and Brooklyn (later Rockville Center) were heavily involved in the membership and work of the CTSA. The theologates of religious communities such as the Jesuits and the Sulpicians continued to be an important part of the CTSA, but the participation of professors from diocesan seminaries was greatly reduced. What explains this phenomenon? One explanation comes from the fact that the CTSA had become much more academic as the years progressed, whereas the orientation of diocesan seminaries was primarily pastoral and not academic. But there is another important factor. As will be developed later in great depth, the CTSA from 1971 to 1995 became identified with the acceptance and support of theological dissent from noninfallible Church teaching. Diocesan seminaries with their mission of training diocesan priests tended to be very supportive of papal teaching and all of its ramifications. A different ecclesial ethos thus existed in the CTSA that was not present in diocesan seminaries.

As the society grew in numbers, there was also a need for some restructuring of the leadership because more responsibilities began to exist. From the beginning, there was a president and a vice president, each of whom served for one year, and a secretary and treasurer who had longer terms. In 1982, the constitution was revised to include three officers—president, president-elect, and vice president. The vice president would succeed to the two presidential offices so that the only contested election each year would be for the vice president. In practice, a primary role for the newly founded office of the president-elect was to plan the convention for that year (1982, 189–90). A committee was appointed to find someone to fill the newly activated office of executive secretary. The president, on the recommendation of the committee in 1981, appointed Michael McGinniss of La Salle University for a five-year term as executive secretary. The executive secretary would take over some of the existing responsibilities of the secretary and the treasurer, and the business office of the society would be transferred to the office of the executive secretary (1991, 211–12).

The meetings in the course of the time frame from 1971 to 1995 continued to have the same basic structure as found in the past—a convention liturgy, greeting from the local bishop or his representative, plenary sessions, some breakout sessions, a business meeting involving the admission of new members, the election of officers and the board, reports from the various officers and new business, including resolutions, as well as the presidential address.

The size of the meetings grew with the growth in membership. By the 1990s, upwards of four hundred were attending the annual conventions. The fiftieth anniversary meeting in New York at the same Commodore Hotel (but with a new name) as the original 1946 meeting drew 576 registrations (1995, 320). This was the best attended meeting in the fifty-year history of the CTSA. The fact that it was the fiftieth anniversary meeting and that it met in New York helped to explain the record attendance.

As the number of people attending the meetings grew, so did the number of sessions on the program. A comparison of the 1971 meeting with the 1990 meeting will give a flavor of how the meetings evolved. The theme of the 1971 convention was "The Impact of American Culture and Experience on Theology." The meeting began on Tuesday, June 15, with two plenary sessions—Joseph Sittler of the University of Chicago on "An Aspect of American Religious Experience" and John H. Wright of the Jesuit School of Theology in Berkeley on "Meaning and Characteristics of an American Theology." Each paper was followed by one respondent. There were four breakout sessions during the convention, each with three different groups and a session involving seven discussion seminars. Richard A. McCormick gave the presidential address. In earlier times, the breakout sessions involved various aspects of the theological discipline, such as fundamental, dogmatic, moral, sacramental, and spiritual theology. In 1971, however, many of the breakout sessions were related to the theme of the convention—or example, Christology in the Contemporary American Scene, American History, American History and Contemporary Theology, Religious Life in America, and The Influence of American Youth. In addition, there were other more general theological issues, such as the resurrection as a historical event, the theological position of the state of Israel, and the relationship of the empirical sciences to moral theology. Of note in the second category is the discussion of Lawrence Lucas's book *Black Priest/White Church*.

There were both basic continuity and some change in the convention formats in the ensuing twenty-five years. The conventions retained the basic structure of plenary and breakout sessions. Each convention addressed a particular theme, and the theme influenced both the plenary and some of the breakout sessions. A new feature of the breakout sessions was the formation of interest groups, which in some ways related to the earlier groups based on the different subjects within the discipline of theology such as Christology, spirituality, moral theology. But now the interest groups were much more specific than just the general topics such as Trinity or Christology. These interest groups were formed by those interested in the particular topic. The group had to get approval from the board. They existed for a term and were discontinued if they failed to attract enough members. These interest groups brought people with the same topical concerns together to discuss the issue.

The 1990 convention gives a good example of how the conventions were structured near the end of this twenty-five-year time frame. The theme of the 1990 convention was "Inculturation and Catholicity." The three plenary sessions addressed inculturation and Catholicity in the early Church, in North America, and in the worldwide Church. Anne Patrick, the president, further developed the convention theme in regard to social justice. (Since the president-elect was responsible for proposing the theme, the presidential address did not always reflect the convention theme.) The breakout sessions were of two types—workshops and continuing seminars. Many workshops carried out the convention theme. The president-elect invited some of these, but the majority were proposed by members in keeping with the convention theme. Sixteen different workshops met on two occasions during this 1990 convention. Topics included how inculturation influenced various topics such as Mary, preaching, and eschatology. Some workshops addressed the role of minorities in North America and considered not only the "larger minorities" such as Blacks and Hispanics but also Francophones, native peoples, East Asians, and Eastern Christians. There were thirteen continuing seminars that met twice during the convention. They included some of the topic areas of theology, such as Christology, Trinity, moral theology, and spirituality, as well as more specific areas, such as North American theology, comparative theology, and the American Catholic experience. At the 1990 banquet, the John Courtney Murray Award was given. It was only in 1980 that the practice began of giving the award at the convention banquet (1980, 315). Before that time, it was often given at the business meeting.

At the 1993 meeting, the board set up a committee to review the structure of the conventions, concerning especially the breakout sessions, and asked the membership to fill out a questionnaire about this possible restructuring. A committee chaired by Kenneth Himes was appointed with all the members having been active in the society and having held elected office. The purposes of this review committee included the following: to establish more democratic processes allowing more members to participate in the convention; to relieve the president-elect of some responsibilities of planning the convention; to establish a greater variety of formal categories for the meeting (recall there were two existing categories: workshops and continuing seminars); to ensure that the number of sessions matches the number of meeting rooms available at the particular hotel. The committee reported to the board at their October 1992 meeting and received suggestions from the board, and the board ultimately approved the revised structure at the 1993 June meeting. This structure went into full effect at the 1995 meeting.

There are different kinds of breakout sessions. Those designated "continuing" have program space until the whole program structure is reviewed. "Developing" groups are reviewed annually. "Select" sessions are selected by the program committee from proposals made by the members. "Invitational" sessions are invited by the president-elect. A "research" group approved by the program committee has a three-year term (1997, 179).

The business meeting of the CTSA, like all societies, had a place for new business. As the 1970s continued, this time often saw the request for the membership to approve resolutions on particular actions, often related to the internal life of the Church itself, but also including sometimes political and social issues. The problems with this procedure came to the fore at the 1978 meeting in Milwaukee. This business meeting began at eleven o'clock on Saturday morning with the presidential address scheduled immediately afterward. President Agnes Cunningham was in the chair when the issue of new business began. The following resolution was made from the floor and seconded: "Be it resolved that the CTSA, with no intention of judging the content and substance of his work, hereby notes its dissatisfaction at the lack of due process in the silencing of Rev. John McNeill SJ."

John McNeill, in 1976, had published *The Church and the Homosexual*, in which he argued in favor of the morality of committed homosexual relationships. The Congregation for the Doctrine of the Faith condemned the teaching found in his book, removed the imprimatur that had been granted the book by the Jesuit Superior, and forbade McNeill from teaching about the issue. McNeill accepted his silencing.[1]

The discussion at the close of the business meeting was heated and drawn out. At first, a motion to table was accepted by a show of hands. A second motion expressed the CTSA's concern about the McNeill case and asked for further information. According to the minutes of the meeting, before the exact wording of this motion could be worked out, the motion was defeated by a show of hands. Then, a motion was made to reconsider the original motion, and this time it was passed by a show of hands. Then a motion was made to adjourn the business meeting in order to have the presidential address, since it was already after 12:30. The discussion had been chaotic and heated, the time was late, and President Cunningham was visibly distraught by the whole situation. She then decided not to give her presidential address. Thus, because of the prolonged discussion over the resolution, the first woman president of the CTSA was unable to give her presidential address (1978, 274).

Something had to be done for a more orderly way of proposing resolutions. The board discussed ways to deal with this problem at the 1979 meeting, calling for resolutions to be submitted before the meeting (1979, 237). The process was modified at the 1995 meeting with a new committee on resolutions. Proposed resolutions should be sent to the committee fifteen days before the convention, and if approved by the committee, they would be placed on the agenda of the convention. The committee would hold a session before the business meeting to discuss the resolutions. Resolutions could be proposed at the business meeting itself if approved by one-third of the members at the meeting (1995, 219). At the 1980 meeting, Agnes Cunningham was given a special award in honor of her ten years of service on the board of directors and as president of the society (1980, 318). One can only surmise that Catholic guilt feelings over the fact that she was not able to give her presidential address two years before were the reason behind this special award.

Research Projects

A particularly important aspect of the second twenty-five-year period of the CTSA was the establishment and work of research projects. By 1970, the CTSA had been involved in a few projects with others, but President McCormick in 1971 began the work of research projects funded by the society. To help support such projects, McCormick sent a letter to all the bishops asking for their financial support. These letters continued for many years and supported the research projects. The three proposed research projects in 1971 dealt with the new code of medical ethics, pastoral activity concerning the divorced and remarried, and the theological implications of the ecumenical dialogue between the Catholic Church and other communions. At the 1972 meeting, the board voted unanimously to accept the reports of these committees without expressing agreement or disagreement with the contents; to publish the reports in the 1972 *Proceedings*; and to encourage independent publication of the reports, thus bringing about greater discussion (1972, 179).

The document on healthcare ethics is a critical evaluation of the *Ethical and Religious Directives for Catholic Health Facilities* approved by the U.S. bishops at their November 1971 meeting. The CTSA committee report emphasizes the greater pluralism now existing with regard to Catholic hospitals in terms of staff, patients, and funding. The document seeks to avoid two extremes. The one extreme is a code that might violate the rights of non-Catholics, harm the social good, and force the closing of some Catholic hospitals. The other extreme to be avoided is to merely accept what is done in other hospitals, claim no Catholic identity, and totally accept secularized values (1972, 248). Two approaches are proposed to avoid such extremes. The first proposal comes from the preamble of the Canadian Catholic *Medical-Moral Guide*. Note that this is called a guide and not a code. The preamble says that the guidelines should serve to enhance the judgment of conscience, not to replace it (1972, 255). The second approach is to incorporate the principle of doubt found in the 1955 edition of the *Directives* but not found in the 1971 *Directives*. In questions legitimately debated by theologians, liberty and the possibility of diversity exist. The report in this context explicitly endorses the legitimate right to dissent from noninfallible hierarchical and papal teaching in certain circumstances (1972, 241–69).

The committee on the problem of second marriages considers two aspects of the question. In the light of contemporary conditions, many Catholic marriages break down. A good number, but by no means all, of these marriages from a moral perspective might be invalid from the beginning, but this cannot always be proved legally in the forum of the Church tribunals. The committee concludes that a negative decision from the tribunal does not close the issue morally. The report provides criteria to be used in the formation of the conscience of the individual in this situation to enter a second marriage. The Christian community and its representatives should respect the conscientious decision made by the individual in this case, neither approving nor disapproving it. The difference between the legal order and the moral order has often been recognized in the Church.

The second aspect of the question concerns participation in the sacramental life of the Church for those already in second, invalid marriages. For the reasons mentioned above, some of these second marriages might in the eyes of God not correspond with their status of being illegal. In other situations, it might be morally wrong to terminate the relationship (e.g., because of children). If a couple, after prayerful consideration of all the realities involved, concludes in conscience that they are worthy to participate in the Eucharist, their judgment should be respected. If explained properly, there should be no scandal resulting from such judgments (1992, 230–40).

The third research proposal established in the 1971 meeting involves a theological review and critique of the bilateral consultations between the Ecumenical and Interreligious Affairs Committee of the National Conference of Catholic

Bishops with eight Christian denominations or communions. The committee studied especially the official reports and consensus statements coming from these eight different conversations. The document is a lengthy, detailed study, which is impossible to summarize in a short space. The committee evaluation included recommendations for giving directions for future dialogues (1972, 179–232).

The CTSA saw these research projects as part of the ongoing work of the society in presenting a scholarly, theological voice expressing Roman Catholic positions, reflection, or evaluation on questions in the public forum. Encouraged by the success of the first three research projects, two new committees were established after the 1972 convention dealing with the renewal of the sacrament of penance and human sexuality. Once again, the president continued the custom of seeking contributions from the U.S. bishops to support these research projects (1972, 174). On Wednesday evening of the 1973 convention, there were forums to discuss these first three research projects (1973, 298). In 1974, as mentioned earlier, President McBrien asked Joseph Nearon to head a research project on Black theology. At the 1974 meeting, Nearon gave a pre-preliminary report (1974, 413–17). At the 1974 convention, on Thursday morning there was a report and discussion of these three research projects on penance, sexuality, and Black theology (1974, 421). The minutes of the 1975 convention report that the research project on penance was finished. The committee on sexuality had finished the first draft of what would be a book-length manuscript. A summary was published in the *Proceedings*. In the coming years, the research project on Black theology would continue and a new project on women in the Church was organized (1975, 257).

In 1991, the board approved a committee to write a book for the fiftieth anniversary of the CTSA in 1995. Robert Wister, a church historian from Seton Hall University, was to write a basic history of about seventy pages, while others would contribute individual essays (1991, 210; 1994, 233). Unfortunately, the project never came to fruition. Wister, however, was able to publish four very short reports—CTSA Firsts, CTSA Presidents, CTSA Award Winners, and Membership Analysis in the *Proceedings* of the fiftieth anniversary convention in 1995 (1995, 293–305). The last page of the Membership Analysis is a one-page table of the fifteen research projects produced from 1972 to 1990. Six of these resulted in books. The number and size of these reports make it impossible to discuss all of them here. The description here of the first few projects illustrates what this whole project intended to do. The next section in this chapter will deal with the major tension experienced in the life of the society during this twenty-five-year period—the relationship between the papal magisterium and theologians. Five or more of the research projects dealt with this tension and will be considered in the following section. For now, it is sufficient to conclude this section on research projects with a table put together by Robert Wister (1995, 305).

	Topic	Chair	Published
1972	Bilateral Consultations I	Avery Dulles	*Proceedings* 27: 179–232
1972	Catholic Hospital Ethics	Warren Reich	*Proceedings* 27: 241–69
1972	Problem of Second Marriages	John Connery	*Proceedings* 27: 233–40
1974	Black Theology: Preliminary	Joseph Nearon	*Proceedings* 29: 413–18
1975	Renewal of Sacrament of Penance	Kenan Osborne	Book by CTSA
1975	Human Sexuality: Summary	Anthony Kosnik	*Proceedings* 30:221–38

	Topic	Chair	Published
1977	Human Sexuality	Anthony Kosnik	Book by Paulist Press
1978	Women in Church and Society	Sara Butler	Book by CTSA
1979	Bilateral Consultations II	Richard McBrien	*Proceedings* 34: 253–85
1980	Cooperation between Theologians and the Church's Teaching Authority	Leo O'Donovan	*Proceedings* 35: 325–36
1982	Cooperation between Theologians and the Ecclesiastical Magisterium	Leo O'Donovan	Book by CTSA and CLSA
1984	Doctrinal Responsibilities	Leo O'Donovan	*Proceedings* 39: 209–34 and CLSA *Proceedings* 45 (1983): 261–84
1986	Approval of Catechisms and Catechetical Materials	John Boyle	*Proceedings* 41: 181–204. Joint comm.: CTSA, CTS, CLSA, NCDDRE
1986	Catholic Perspectives on Baptism, Eucharist, and Ministry	Michael Fahey	Book by University Press of America
1990	Profession of Faith/Oath of Fidelity	Michael Buckley	Book by CTSA

Predominant Tension

There is no doubt that the predominant tension in the life of the CTSA from 1971 to 1995 was the relationship between theologians and the hierarchical magisterium. This section will discuss this relationship as found in the business meetings of the society and in the pertinent research projects.

From the beginning of this time frame in 1971, the society (not every individual member) was identified with the legitimacy of dissent under certain circumstances from noninfallible papal teaching. At this time, Richard McCormick and myself were recognized as the two leading figures in the United States supporting such dissent. As noted earlier, I was the elected president of the CTSA in 1970, not, however, without opposition, and McCormick served as president in 1971. Also, as pointed out earlier, one of the first research projects of the society on guidelines for medical ethics in Catholic healthcare institutions supported such dissent.

At the 1971 meeting, the assembly passed a resolution urging the executive committee of the U.S. bishops to reconsider their decision excluding those who have been dispensed from the obligation from celibacy from serving as staff or consultants on projects of the National Conference of Catholic Bishops. In addition, the meeting supported a resolution coming from the board suggesting to Cardinal John Dearden, the head of the U.S. bishops, the consideration of official theological representation at national and regional meetings of the bishops (1971, 256). In 1974, this convention passed a resolution in conjunction with the College Theology Society and proposed by the board that laicization itself should not be a barrier to functioning as a theologian in Catholic schools, colleges, and universities. An amendment to add the word *seminaries* was defeated (1971, 436). In 1975, a CTSA committee on consultation concerning the draft of the

National Catechetical Directory noted some significant problems with this draft (1975, 257).

The beginning of the research project on human sexuality has been mentioned. The final report itself had multiple important consequences, including for the life of the CTSA itself. A summary of the four-hundred-page report appeared in the 1975 *Proceedings* (1975, 221–37). At the next meeting, it was reported that the board had received the final draft of the sexuality report from Anthony Kosnik, the committee chair (1976, 255–56). According to the 1977 minutes, the human sexuality report was received and sent to two moral theologians and a social scientist for a critique, and these recommendations and those of the board were sent back to the committee (1977, 253).

Paulist Press published the book after the 1977 meeting. The title page gives the title *Human Sexuality: A Study Commissioned by the Catholic Theological Society of America*, together with the authors, beginning with the chair of the committee (Anthony Kosnik) and the other four committee members. After three chapters on Scripture, tradition, and the social sciences, the book develops the basic moral principle that sexuality involves a creative growth toward integration. This basic principle is then spelled out in seven fundamental values: self-liberation, enrichment of the other, honesty, fidelity, service to life, social responsibility, and joy. On the basis of these values, the book develops guidelines—not norms because they admit of some exceptions— for sexual activity. Many of these disagree with the magisterial teaching. Even when there is general agreement with such magisterial teaching, *Human Sexuality* recognizes the possibility of some exceptions.

The report of the committee, like the previous proposals, was received by the board without approval or disapproval. However, since it was a study commissioned by the CTSA, it was very much associated with the society. No other work of the society has received as much publicity, both in the secular press and media and in the Catholic press. The Doctrinal Committee of the U.S. bishops in November 1977 deemed the book to be misguided, theologically weak, and unfit for use by pastoral counselors.[2] The bishops took no action against the authors, but later Anthony Kosnik was removed from his position as professor of moral theology at the St. Cyril and Methodius Seminary in Orchard Lake, Michigan. The Congregation for the Doctrine of the Faith on July 13, 1979, issued a strong critique of the book. The congregation also expressed the concern that a distinguished society of Catholic theologians would have arranged for the publication of this report in such a way as to give broad distribution to the erroneous principles and conclusions of this book and in this way provide a source of confusion among the people of God.[3]

This book was also the final reason for some members of the CTSA and other Catholic academics to form a new society—the Fellowship of Catholic Scholars. According to the self-understanding of this fellowship, three recent developments precipitated the establishment of this group—the negative reaction to *Humanae vitae*, the publication of the book *Human Sexuality*, and the Land O'Lakes Statement on Catholic higher education. A small group of six met in May 1977. A subsequent meeting of many others in August 1977 decided to form the Fellowship of Catholic Scholars. The first meeting was held in April 1978, and the fellowship continues to have annual meetings and some publications. Its purposes include accepting as a rule of life and thought the entire faith of the Catholic Church as found not merely in solemn definitions but also in the ordinary teaching of the pope and those bishops in union with the pope. Those who apply for membership must be approved.[4] Some members of the fellowship retained their membership in the CTSA, but most identified only with the fellowship. Thus, there was no longer one society where all Catholic theologians would come together to discuss their work.

The 1977 *Proceedings* included a preconvention seminar by John Farrelly criticizing the methodology employed in *Human Sexuality* (1977, 221–33). At the business meeting, a motion to accept the statement of the board found in the beginning of *Human Sexuality* that the board neither approved nor disapproved passed. A motion to ask the publisher to remove from the title page and the jacket the phrase "A Study Commissioned by the CTSA" was defeated by a voice vote (1977, 254). In the 1978 meeting, Daniel Maguire gave a paper strongly supporting the book. Cathleen Going and William Everett responded to Maguire's presentation (1978, 54–90).

Several issues involving theologians and the magisterium came up in the 1980 meeting. A committee chaired by Leo O'Donovan was appointed in 1979 to come up with possibilities for a more cooperative and constructive relationship between theologians and Church teaching authority. In response to the O'Donovan committee's suggestion, the board proposed a joint committee established by the CTSA and the Canon Law Society of America (CLSA) to develop a set of norms to guide the resolution of difficulties between theologians and the teaching authority. At the business meeting in 1980, the members unanimously voted to accept the board's proposal to set up such a joint committee with the CLSA (1980, 322). The first part of the report of the joint committee was published in 1982. It contained six papers with a theologian and a canonist addressing three issues—the rights and responsibilities of bishops, the rights and responsibilities of theologians, and evaluation of current procedures. A final consensus statement concluded this first phase of the report.[5]

Also, at the 1980 meeting, the president reported several exchanges he had with the Congregation for the Doctrine of the Faith and other interested parties about *Human Sexuality*, the interrogation of Dutch theologian Edward Schillebeeckx, and the action taken against Hans Küng. Also, the board had set up a committee to make a report on *Sapientia Christiana*, the apostolic constitution of John Paul II insisting on hierarchical control of theologians teaching in pontifical schools and faculties (i.e., those that grant academic degrees accredited by the Vatican). The committee report was received by the board and circulated to all the membership. It was published in the *Proceedings* and in *The Jurist*. No other specific action was contemplated by the board. However, the report itself does not appear in the online version of the *Proceedings*. The 1980 meeting also passed in a voice vote a resolution from the floor calling for the elimination of the requirement of a canonical mission for professors of Catholic theology in the proposed Code of Canon Law (1980, 323).

The 1981 *Proceedings* report that a letter was sent to some fifty concerned agencies expressing the very serious concern of the CTSA about the requirement for a canonical mission for all who teach theology or related disciplines in all Catholic institutions of higher learning in the new proposed revision of the Code of Canon Law (1981, 198). The obvious fear behind such a concern is that the legitimate role of the theologian will be unduly restricted by Church authorities. James Coriden proposed a resolution that the CTSA make strong representation to Archbishop Joseph Bernardin, the general secretary of the U.S. bishops' conference, of our grave concern about the requirement of a canonical mission for those who teach theology in Catholic institutions of higher learning in the proposed revision of Canon Law. Of 168 active members voting, only two voted no. It was suggested that this figure also be reported to Archbishop Bernardin (1981, 199–200).

At the 1982 meeting, the board proposed a resolution that speakers at the joint colloquia sponsored by the Joint Committee of Catholic Learned Societies and Scholars (JCCLSS) and the bishops' Committee on Doctrine not be subject to veto by either party. The dialogue with the Committee on Doctrine was now carried on through the JCCLSS and not just by the CTSA alone. The proposed resolution passed on a voice vote by the assembly (1982, 194).

The elections at the 1983 meeting showed the membership's support for Anthony Kosnik. Four others were nominated by the nominating committee for the board; Kosnik was nominated from the floor and was the first new board member elected. For our purposes, the most significant action taken by the 1983 convention concerns the second and final phase of the report of the joint committee of the CTSA and the CLSA on Cooperation between Theologians and the Ecclesiastical Magisterium. The report published in the 1984 *Proceedings* has three parts. Part 1 presents a general description of the ecclesial framework, the operative principles, and the responsibilities of bishops and theologians. Part 2, "Structuring Cooperation," recommends ways in which bishops and theologians can build a spirit of cooperation, especially through personal contact and informal dialogue. Part 3, "Formal Doctrinal Dialogue," sets out a procedure to deal with doctrinal disputes between bishops and theologians in dioceses. Since the circumstances in the nearly two hundred dioceses differ widely, the procedures are flexible so as to be adaptable to local needs and conditions. In some circumstances, regional rather than diocesan structured dialogue might be more appropriate. This structured dialogue comes into play if collaboration has not been able to solve the problem. Such dialogue is not a judicial or administrative process. This dialogue should take place before considering any exercise of administrative authority in regard to doctrinal matters. The purpose of the dialogue is to determine the nature and gravity, as well as the pastoral implications, of the issue in dispute. This elaborate and detailed process spells out four steps—gathering the data, clarifying the meaning, determining the relationship with Catholic tradition, identifying the implications for the life of the Church. The aim of this doctrinal dialogue is to resolve the issue, but despite the best attempts, there might be need for subsequent administrative action. Administrative actions do not resolve doctrinal issues but rather address pastoral situations. Such sanctions should be proportionate to the pastoral requirements of the common good and shall be no more severe than those requirements demand (1984, 209–30).

In my judgment, the procedures are well done and procedurally sound, but they do not deal with the existential reality. The real problem arises not on the local level but when the Congregation for the Doctrine of the Faith (CDF) takes the initiative. In the best of all worlds, problems should first be handled on the local level, but the Church reality at this time shows the real controversial issues come from the intervention of the CDF. Perhaps this report implicitly recognizes such a problem, because it adds an appendix analyzing and criticizing the procedures of the CDF as found in the *Ratio agendi* document. In very diplomatic language, the report states that the existing procedures can be improved in many ways. In keeping with the principle of subsidiarity, the CDF should refer any complaint about unorthodoxy to the local bishop. Every attempt at resolution should be attempted before the matter is brought back to the CDF. The report then makes ten proposals for more just procedures in the processes of the CDF (1984, 230–32).

The CTSA board not only received this report but endorsed it and asked the membership at the 1983 meeting to endorse it. The membership at the meeting unanimously accepted that the report Doctrinal Responsibilities be recommended as a working document to the National Conference of Bishops for promoting cooperation and resolving disputes between bishops and theologians (1983, 148).

Another resolution passed at that same meeting contrasted with the report Doctrinal Responsibilities. The statement concerned the situation of Sister Mary Agnes Mansour, who was the head of social services for the state of Michigan. The Vatican decreed that she either had to resign from her job because it involved financial support for abortions or else be relieved of her vows as a Sister of Mercy. The statement of the board was discussed and amended at the regular business meeting and a second special meeting. The resolution passed by voice vote begins by mentioning that the actions of the Holy See that have led to the resignation of Sister Mary Agnes Mansour from the Sisters of Mercy have theological dimensions of profound concern to the Catholic Theological Society of America. As a result, "we strongly support serious dialogue about the underlying issues raised by this case." This revised conclusion softens what had initially been proposed by the board—"We strongly support speedy reconsideration of this regrettable decision" (1983, 148–50).[6] The juxtaposition of these two issues points out the problem mentioned above. Very often the Vatican begins the process bypassing all the other three levels. Subsidiarity unfortunately is not a vital principle in Church life at this time. At the 1984 meeting, the president reported he sent last year's resolution regarding the Mary Agnes Mansour case to all those involved in it, but all he received were several acknowledgments of having received his letter (1984, 203–4).

The board at two different meetings during the 1984 convention discussed the recent withdrawals of the imprimatur from books. No names were mentioned, but the two best-known cases concerned the popular catechism *Christ among Us* written by Anthony Wilhelm and Philip Keane's *Sexual Morality*.[7] The president took a number of steps, including setting up an advisory committee to discuss the matter with the doctrinal committee of the U.S. bishops (1984, 205). At the 1985 convention, the ad hoc committee on imprimaturs was expanded to a joint committee with other interested societies and was called to work with the bishops' committee to decide the criteria applicable to the evaluation of catechetical works (1985, 222). This committee wrote a long report that was published in the *Proceedings* of the 1986 convention (1986, 181–204). The report discussed different types of catechetical materials and the process of approval granted by the corresponding Church authority.

The 1986 *Proceedings* also include the response of the CTSA to the 1986 draft document of the Congregation for Education entitled "Proposed Schema (Draft) for a Pontifical Document on Catholic Universities" (1986, 205–8). The CTSA board's statement is very critical of the proposed document. The document in its present form would do serious damage to the Church in North America. In light of the great diversity in Catholic higher education throughout the world, greater attention must be paid to these significant differences. Without explicitly saying so, the CTSA board's report fears Vatican control over what takes place in higher educational institutions regarding theology and related disciplines in North America.

At the 1986 business meeting, the board presented a resolution to the assembly that for the good of Roman Catholic theology, Catholic higher education, and the Catholic Church in North America, "we strongly urge that no action be taken against Charles Curran that would prohibit him from teaching on the theology faculty of the Catholic University of America." To prepare for this proposal, an "informational session" was held on the previous evening with several speakers both pro and con. After discussion at the business meeting, the resolution was adopted overwhelmingly by a show of hands. A call for a count of the vote showed: Yes, 171; No, 14; Abstain, 4.

To understand better this resolution, some historical context is necessary. In the summer of 1979, I was informed in a letter from Cardinal Franjo Seper, the prefect of the CDF, that I was under investigation and asked to respond to sixteen pages of observations. The correspondence with the CDF continued in the ensuing years. A September 17, 1985, letter from Cardinal Joseph Ratzinger, who had succeeded Seper as prefect of the CDF, asked me to reconsider and retract my positions on contraception, sterilization, abortion and euthanasia, masturbation, premarital sexuality, and the indissolubility of marriage. If I did not retract, I could no longer be called a Catholic theologian. Cardinal Ratzinger agreed to meet with me in an informal meeting in Rome on March 8. The meeting did not result in any breakthrough as both sides defended their own positions. We did agree, however, that the Vatican would issue a press release saying the meeting had occurred. Upon returning to Washington, I held a press conference to address the matter on the next day. Both the secular and religious press and media gave considerable coverage to the controversy. The only other occasion that the CDF had declared someone not to be a Catholic theologian was the case of Hans Küng in Germany. Even before the June 1986 CTSA meeting, with the assistance of a student support group at CUA, a letter supporting me signed by a number of former presidents of the CTSA and the CTS had been sent out to the membership of both societies. This letter strongly defended me and urged that no action be taken. The letter was ultimately signed by more than 750 Catholic theologians.[8]

The board, with an acute political sense, proposed another resolution at the 1986 meeting. In support of the U.S. bishops' efforts to develop "a consistent ethic of life," the board urged members in their research, writing, and teaching to work resolutely on the development of such an ethic. The wording supports the need to develop a consistent ethic of life but does not endorse the position taken by the U.S. bishops. The motion was adopted overwhelmingly (1986, 177).

My specific case came up again in the three subsequent meetings. At the 1987 convention, the president gave a detailed report on "the Curran Affair" (1987, 196–99). The president communicated the resolution from last year to Cardinal Ratzinger. In accord with CUA statutes, I requested a due process hearing by a faculty committee to determine if Chancellor Hickey, on the basis of the judgment of the CDF approved by the pope that I was neither suitable nor eligible to be a Catholic theologian, could take away my canonical mission to teach theology there. The board of the CTSA at the October 1986 meeting sent a statement supporting me to the CUA board of inquiry. The statement was sent to all CTSA members who were invited individually and corporately in their respective departments or faculties to endorse the statement and send their endorsements to the CUA committee. The response was very great. At its June 1987 meeting, the membership endorsed the statement of the board. It was a very strong testimony of support that concluded, "Removing him from his teaching position is incomprehensible on professional grounds, unjust in the singling out of this one scholar from many of his peers with similar opinions, and indefensible in the light of the traditional understanding of what a theologian rightly does." The president and vice president attended the faculty hearing at CUA as official CTSA observers.

To complete the narrative, Chancellor Hickey did not accept the conclusion of the faculty committee that I should be permitted to teach at CUA in my area of competency, otherwise the canonical mission should not be removed.[9] At the 1988 convention, in light of the reality that I was going to be removed from CUA, the membership deplored such action and reaffirmed its conviction that my teaching theology at CUA serves well the good of theology, of Catholic higher education, and of the Church itself (1988, 187). The 1989 *Proceedings* mentions the statement of President John Boyle of March 2, 1989, on the secular court decision concerning Charles Curran. (The federal district court of the District of Columbia decided in favor of the CUA in dismissing me, because there was nothing in my contract or any other faculty member's contract that would guarantee that the university would always come down on the side of academic freedom in a conflict with the Vatican.[10]) The 1989 meeting endorsed the president's statement, but the *Proceedings* did not publish that statement (1989, 186).

The 1987 convention was informed that the bishops' Committee on Doctrine had accepted with only slight modifications the report Doctrinal Responsibilities from the joint CTSA-CSLA committee. Information was also provided about the early work on the intersocietal committee on academic freedom. The committee on resolutions proposed a resolution on academic freedom that supported legitimate academic freedom but did not endorse the American Association of University Professors' (AAUP) documents because of the complexities of the different settings of CTSA members. It asked the board to take further steps to study this matter and report back at the June 1988 meeting. The resolution passed by a clear show of hands (1987, 198). The different settings obviously refers to seminaries.

The resolutions committee proposed two resolutions at the 1988 meeting. The first resolution, in light of the growing urgent problems confronting theologians, reaffirmed the support for the joint CTSA-CLSA report Doctrinal Responsibilities, expressed appreciation for the work of the Joint Committee of Catholic Learned Societies and Scholars for its work of fostering relationships between bishops and theologians, and directed the leadership of the CTSA to suggest ways in which episcopal responsibility and academic competence can work in harmony. The resolution was accepted on a voice vote. A second resolution endorsing the AAUP documents on academic freedom was tabled (1988, 185–86). The report of the Intersocietal Committee on Academic Freedom and Ecclesial Responsibility was published in the 1988 *Proceedings*. The committee is convinced that many of its member societies (Catholic Biblical Association,

CTSA, and CTS) are disheartened by restrictions imposed on some of their colleagues and points out the problem posed for the Church by mistrust of its scholars and disregard of their scholarly expertise. The committee decided that the best way to fulfill its mandate is to provide a statement of the main issues for the use of the leadership of the three societies (1988, 190–92).

At the 1989 meeting, the president reported on several pertinent issues. The Joint Committee of Catholic Learned Societies and Scholars (JCCLSS) arranged a joint regional conference between bishops and theologians in October 1988 in Los Altos, California, with plans for a second regional meeting in October in Mobile, Alabama. The board had been discussing what action the CTSA might take concerning the Cologne Declaration and similar statements from theologians in other European countries. (The Cologne Declaration signed by 130 German theologians criticized moves to silence left-leaning theologians, the weakening of national conferences of bishops, a narrow interpretation of sexual morality, and the pope's authoritarian ruling style.[11]) There was not enough time for the board to develop a statement of its own on this matter. Later in the business meeting, a resolution proposed from the floor was passed directing the board to propose a statement addressing concerns raised by the Cologne Declaration (1989, 182–83). In the beginning of 1989, the Vatican issued a new Profession of Faith and Oath of Fidelity to be taken by many different people in the Church, including by professors of Catholic theology. The meeting passed a resolution for the board to address the theological and practical issues involved and to direct the president to inform U.S. and Canadian bishops about the CTSA's serious concerns with the profession and the oath (1989, 186).

At the 1990 meeting, the president reported on actions related to the profession and oath. The president in August 1989 appointed a five-person committee chaired by Michael Buckley to respond to the legislation on the profession and oath. They met monthly during the fall and submitted a draft to the board for comments. A final draft was completed by Easter 1990, published, and sent to the membership. The Profession of Faith adds three paragraphs to the older, more general one that had been in place. The most significant of these new paragraphs states, "Moreover, I adhere with the religious *obsequium* of will and intellect to the teachings which either the Roman Pontiff or the college of bishops enunciate when they exercise their authentic Magisterium, even if they do not intend to proclaim these teachings by a definitive act."[12] This paragraph raises the very neuralgic and controversial issue of dissent from such teachings. Many, including myself, argue that "religious *obsequium* of will and intellect" allows for dissent, but the CDF obviously does not agree with this interpretation. Many interpreted this addition once again as a restriction of the legitimate role of Catholic theologians.

The report was a thorough study of 133 pages divided into five parts. The fifth and final part deals with canonical and theological issues raised by this legislation. The final summary points out there are no sanctions in general law for failure to make the Profession of Faith or take the Oath of Fidelity. The report goes on to conclude that it appears appropriate at this time that no action should be taken against those who in conscience cannot make the profession or take the oath in light of the problems surrounding them.[13]

There was much discussion about resolutions concerning this issue in the 1990 business meeting. An amendment was proposed that the CTSA would support the decision of those members who in conscience cannot make the profession or take the oath. This amendment was defeated by a show of hands. That left the other parts of the existing resolution calling for dialogue and discussion with the bishops on the floor. A vote to table this resolution passed on a close vote by a show of hands. Then a resolution from the floor that the CTSA urge its members not to comply with the requirements of the profession and oath was not discussed because it was not accepted for discussion by one-third of the members. But then a resolution was unanimously passed on a voice vote that the membership endorse the document on the Profession of Faith and the Oath of Fidelity (1990, 152–53).

Business meetings do not always develop in a logical way, as well illustrated in this case. Ironically, the original report, which was unanimously affirmed at the end, contains the sentence mentioned above that at this time it is appropriate that no action be taken against those who in conscience cannot make the profession and take the oath. The very lengthy report and the discussion at the business meeting indicate once again the great tensions that continued to exist in the relationship between theologians and the teaching authority.

The 1991 president's report mentions that a final version of the statement occasioned by earlier discussion of the Cologne Declaration was composed by three members of the society and sent to all the members for endorsement. Forty percent responded and, of this 40 percent, 80 percent endorsed the statement. The statement "Do Not Extinguish the Spirit" was also endorsed by the CTS and the Leadership Conference of Women Religious. "Do Not Extinguish the Spirit" was not an official statement of the CTSA but of its many members who signed it (1991, 211). The statement in the context of the twenty-fifth anniversary of the closing of Vatican II discussed four issues—collegiality of bishops, magisterium and theologians, women in the Church, and ecumenism. The document contrasts the hopes found in the documents of Vatican II with the existing realities of the present time.[14] At this meeting, the president also issued a statement in his own name on the new Vatican document "Ecclesial Vocation of Theologians" and made some informal comments about what

84

is happening with the Profession of Faith and Oath of Fidelity (1991, 211).

At the 1992 convention, the board established a committee to study the interpretation and implementation of the Profession of Faith and Oath of Fidelity and to continue the dialogue with bishops and other Church authorities (1992, 190). One resolution from the floor concerned the CDF's "Note" on André Guindon's book *The Sexual Creators,* pointing out serious and fundamental disagreements in the book with the traditional teaching of the Church and recent teachings of the magisterium.[15] The resolution was somewhat curious in asking the CTSA to invite a group of scholars to make a judgment whether the "Note" reflects the principal arguments of the book. The report was not to be approved by the board or the society, but simply sent to the author of the book by December 1, 1992. The resolution passed by a very clear show of hands (1992, 192). Note again the neuralgic area of sexual ethics. The 1993 president's report indicated that the report from those scholars had been sent to Guindon, but the contents of the report were not made public (1993, 185).

The 1993 convention also reported that the CTSA/CLSA/CTS committee on the Profession of Faith continued dialoguing with the bishops' Committee on Doctrine and met on its own to further discuss the issues. "At the present time, it appears that no theologians have been asked to take the profession or the oath" (1993, 184). The 1990 apostolic constitution *Ex corde Ecclesiae* required a mandate (*mandatum*) from the proper Church authority in order to teach theology in a Catholic college or university. To many, this was yet another attempt to control and restrict theologians. A committee of the U.S. bishops sent a draft ordinance to all bishops, to presidents of Catholic colleges and universities, and to Catholic scholarly societies inviting them to submit comments. The CTSA set up a committee to prepare a formal response (1993, 186).

At the 1995 meeting (the fiftieth anniversary of the society), the president reported on the committee dealing with *Ex corde*, which continued the dialogue about how the bishops should respond to this document with its provision that all professors of theology must have a mandate from the proper ecclesiastical authority. Another significant action at this meeting was the society's endorsing the statement of the board based on a special committee report that had already been sent to the individuals involved about the case of Carmel McEnroy. The statement expressed dismay at the dismissal of Carmel McEnroy, RSM, from the faculty of St. Meinrad School of Theology without any due process that the institution itself was committed to follow. Once again, the process for dealing with such disputes found in Doctrinal Responsibilities issued by the National Conference of Catholic Bishops in 1989 was not followed. She was dismissed because, along with many others, she had signed a statement protesting the papal declaration that the Church has no authority to ordain women to the priesthood (1995, 321–22). The 1995 meeting also endorsed the board's document. In addition, the society passed two other resolutions that came from the floor. The first asked the Association of Theological Schools to review what happened to Carmel McEnroy. A second resolution called for her to be reinstated pending the due process procedure (1995, 321–22).

This section has thus demonstrated that the primary tension in the internal life of the CTSA in its second twenty-five-year time frame (1971–95) was the tension between the magisterium and theologians. What explains this tension? The reaction to Pope Paul VI's 1968 encyclical *Humanae vitae* pressed the issue of dissent from noninfallible teachings. Many theologians and others claimed that under John Paul II (1978–2005) the Church became overly centralized in the papacy and failed to follow through on the promises of Vatican II, although not all theologians, including not all members of the CTSA, agreed with this judgment.

The actions of the society were attempts to resist this centralization in general and the efforts to control and discipline theologians who were trying to exercise their rightful role. Throughout this period, the society strongly supported the possibility of dissent but also recognized the legitimate role of bishops in the Church and called for a greater collaboration between bishops and theologians. The tension occasioned the formation of another society called the Fellowship of Catholic Scholars, which insisted on the need for its members to accept the noninfallible teachings of the magisterium.

THEOLOGICAL CONTENT

This section will discuss the theology found in the papers delivered at the CTSA conventions from 1971 to 1995. Although repetitious, it is necessary to note again the impossibility of dealing with all these many papers. More attention will be paid to papers delivered by presidents of the society and Murray Award winners and plenary papers, but my own interests and concerns are bound to have some effect on the matters covered. In light of the long discussion on the primary tension in the inner life of the CTSA in this period, the first topic is the tension between Church authority and theologians. Subsequent areas are the ramifications of the important role that historicity and historical consciousness have played, and the third area is fundamental theology.

Authority and Theologians

The issue of authority and theologians arose primarily in the discussion of the legitimacy of dissent from *Humanae vitae* in 1968. In the 1970 convention, recall that Richard McCormick addressed this issue. The first theologians to speak to this issue were not ecclesiologists but moral theologians, as illustrated in McCormick's 1970 paper on the magisterium. In his presidential address in 1971, McCormick explored the relationship between authority and leadership. Leadership is the capacity to influence the behavior of others in a given situation toward the good of the individual and the common good. Leadership is also a broader notion than juridical authority. But unfortunately, we often tend to equate the two. Leadership can take many different forms, but its goal is to release and stimulate the potential of the individual and the community. The contemporary challenge to authority in the Church is to become leadership (1971, 239–50).

In his 1976 presidential address, "Theologians and Magisterium," Avery Dulles acknowledges the malaise in the Church. Yes, there is a growing collaboration between bishops and theologians, but the relationship is fraught with misunderstandings, tensions, and mistrust. There is truly a crisis in the Church today. In his typical, evenhanded way, Dulles recognizes there are problems with both parties. There are serious problems, however, with the heavily juridicized, neo-Scholastic approach that reduced the wisdom of teaching to obedience to authority, thus denying any possibility of dissent from noninfallible teaching. Dulles appeals to two sources to overcome this overly juridical, neo-Scholastic view. Vatican II itself quietly reversed earlier positions of the magisterium in a number of issues. Second, Thomas Aquinas used the term *magisterium* primarily to describe those teaching in the schools, distinguishing the *officium praelationis* possessed by the bishops with the *officium magisterii* of the professional theologian. For Aquinas, the theologian is a genuine teacher and not just a mouthpiece for higher officers. Thus, there are two magisteria that should be complementary and mutually correcting. The pastoral magisterium has the primary task of the unity of the Church as a community of faith and witness. Many doctrinal questions involve both the protecting of the true faith and also technical theology. In this article, Dulles has tried to strike an alternative model of magisterium different from the neo-Scholastic model (1976, 235–46).

In a 1980 paper, "The Two Magisteria: An Interim Reflection," Dulles describes the qualifications for membership in both magisteria and the functional specialties of each magisterium. In summary, the functional specialty of the ecclesiastical magisterium is judgment; that of the theologian is understanding. The relationship between the two should avoid the extremes of reductionism of the two and the total separation of the two. There should be a dialectical relationship of relative autonomy within mutual acceptance. Both magisteria need one another for the good of each other and the good of the Church (1980, 155–69).

In his 1988 paper, "Magisterium and Theology," Francis Sullivan, then at Boston College and before that at the Gregorian University in Rome, discusses the role of the theologian vis-à-vis infallible dogmatic definitions and noninfallible teaching. In the case of dogmatic definitions, these too need to be interpreted by theologians. Such definitions have a partial nature because they do not relate the statement to all other connected values. The pre–Vatican II understanding had reduced the role of theology to showing how what is defined is contained in revelation. Sullivan appeals to Bernard Lonergan's insistence on historical consciousness, which recognizes that dogmatic statements have meaning in their own contexts, but contexts change over time. Hence, theological interpretation has its role to play. With regard to nondefinitive, noninfallible teaching, such teachings have changed over the years. Such teachings should reflect the best theological opinion of the time, but unfortunately the magisterium has insisted on one school of theology at times and thus creates a problem. Also, theology can develop over time and call for a change in what was taught in a different culture and history.

These insights help us to explain why change has occurred in such noninfallible teaching in the past. Sullivan proposes that the ideal situation would be for the magisterium to admit that the theology has developed and the older noninfallible teaching needs to be changed. But there undoubtedly is great resistance to the magisterium's recognition that its previous teaching has now changed. At the very minimum, the magisterium in the future must avoid the danger of listening to only one school of theology as has happened in some cases in the past (1988, 65–75). Richard McBrien in a response basically supports Sullivan's paper but points out that more might have been said about the role of reception in the Church (1988, 76–79).

Joseph Komonchak of Catholic University in his 1985 paper points out that the relationship between theology and Church authority cannot be seen as only a conversation within the Church, as it was in the pre–Vatican II approach of a countercultural ghetto theology. Theology today must be seen as a mediation between religion and culture. Theology is not an independent first step that is then applied to the existing culture. Theology has an ecclesial and a cultural role. Theology can't just start from a conversation within the Church, but theology and theologians are themselves embedded in their culture. In such an understanding, the ecclesial and cultural roles of theology are not successive moments, but rather simultaneous and dialectically related dimensions of a single hermeneutic practice for which neither theory nor praxis can claim an absolute authority. Hence, theology must avoid the two extremes of being absorbed into the culture or just opposed to the modern culture. In this context, theologians cannot expect Church authority to wait upon the fulfillment of the theological task. The Church and its authority, however, should recognize that theology must be given room to work out its complex task by trial and error with strictly theological criteria and should not attempt to avoid the tensions and dangers of the theological enterprise by an exercise of authority that denies the true role of theology, discourages theologians from undertaking their task, and thus postpones further authentic positions (1985, 15–32).

In my judgment, Komonchak here recognizes the reality of historical consciousness that affects not only the objective reality in its historical development but also the fact that theology itself and the theologian are embedded in culture and that theology is not an essential reality unaffected by the culture in which it exists. Such an appraisal, which is necessary today, further complicates the magisterium-authority relationship.

John P. Boyle of the University of Iowa in his 1979 seminar paper, "The Natural Law and Magisterium," recognizes the many complexities involved in knowing the natural law. He argues against a juridical understanding of the magisterium's role in the teaching of natural law and in favor of a dialogical role involving the different ways of knowing the general aspect of natural law. All human beings, including the nonbaptized, through reason can have this knowledge. The consciences of the Church community have been transfigured by the gift of the Holy Spirit. This is the basis of the important role of reception of magisterial teaching by the whole Church. But the Church community is not merely receptive. The community is the bearer of revelation, and through its experience, the implications of revelation develop in the Church. The Church is a community gifted by the Spirit. The function of the hierarchical magisterium in authoritative teaching of formulating pastoral directives in matters of natural law is one of discernment and articulation helped by the gifts of the Spirit given in ordination. Through the transformation by the Spirit, the Church community and its authoritative teachers can have a prophetic insight into the understanding of natural law, calling attention to implications of natural law that are sometimes neglected. Since all human beings can have an understanding of the implications of natural law, the prophetic role of the Church can hope to illicit a response in the broader human community. Thus, a teaching authority that recognizes the many with competency concerning the natural law will find itself both liberated from pretensions to omniscience and freed for a more modest prophetic role in modern society (1979, 189–210). Thus, Boyle recognizes a dialogical and more modest role for the teaching authority that includes a prophetic role, but this role is dialogical with the total community of the Church and all humankind.

Margaret Farley of Yale University in her 1982 panel paper, "Power and Powerlessness," describes the situation of the Sisters of Mercy of the Union, who sponsor the largest group of private hospitals in the country, in a conflict with Church authority over the magisterial teaching that tubal ligation is morally wrong and should not be done in Catholic institutions. After much dialogue and study, the general administration of the Sisters of Mercy recommended that their hospitals do tubal ligations when they are determined to be for the good of the patient. Their recommendation was counter to the Ethical Directives for Catholic Hospitals promulgated by the U.S. bishops. Dialogue started between the sisters and a committee of the U.S. bishops on this issue. However, the pope and the Roman curia then intervened to determine if the administrative team of the Sisters of Mercy accepted the teaching of the magisterium and would withdraw their letter to the hospitals. The administrative team submitted to the demand to be silenced and withdrew their letter to the hospitals but insisted they still held to their position as true. They agreed to be silenced in order that their voices and their understanding of the truth would ultimately prevail. They were powerless when confronted with the power of Church authority. The danger, as Farley pointed out, is that power would ultimately have the last word (1982, 116–19). Farley's case study well illustrates the problem of a juridical approach to Church teaching, as well as the unfortunate situation of the powerlessness of women in our Church.

This section has dealt with the theological understanding of authority in the Church and specifically the relationship between the magisterium and theology, which was earlier shown to be the primary tension experienced in the internal life of the society.

Historicity

The focus will now be on historicity and historical consciousness and its application in the theological life of the Church in this time frame. Recall that John Courtney Murray appealed to history and historical development to criticize the thesis method of doing theology and to propose the need for the Church to accept religious freedom. The reform of Vatican II was based on *ressourcement*, a return to the sources, and *aggiornamento*, bringing the Church up to date by dialoguing with the modern world. Bernard Lonergan maintained that the most far-reaching change in Vatican II that affected its whole approach was the shift from classicism to historical consciousness. Historical consciousness recognizes not only historical development in the objective order but also that the subject and theologians themselves are embedded in their own particular times and cultures.

Francis Sullivan appealed to Lonergan's understanding of historical consciousness in developing the role of theology vis-à-vis the teaching of the magisterium. This emphasis on historicity, historical development, and historical consciousness in the second twenty-five-year period in the life of the CTSA (1971–95) helps to explain three significant aspects of CTSA papers at this time—the important role of experience; recognition of the need for an American theology; and aspects of liberation theology, beginning with the experience of the poor.

The role of experience

The understanding of experience in the light of historicity and historical consciousness is well illustrated in the paper of Ellen Leonard of the University of St. Michael's College Toronto at the 1988 convention, "Experience as a Source for Theology" (1988, 44–61). She understands experience in the way it is generally taken. Leonard agrees with Monika Hellwig about the shift in contemporary theology that the recovery of present experience in its full social and political dimensions is foundational. As a result, it is necessary to correct the bias in the past understanding of experience. The past is not ignored, but the past must be appropriated by the present community in the light of present experiences and concerns.

There is now a need to correct the biases and past experiences that ignored many experiences in our present situation. Theology today is being transformed as persons and communities previously overlooked or externally defined reflect on their experience of particularity. There are many significant and different experiences that exist today. Past experience failed to recognize these minority voices. The older understanding thought there was only one experience that all shared. But this was the experience of those in power. Traditional Western theology is culture-bound, Church-centered, male-dominated, age-dominated, pro-capitalist, anti-Communist, nonrevolutionary, and overly theoretical. Here Leonard is citing Tissa Balasuriya. What has been presented as "human experience" in the past is now seen to be limited, distorted, and in need of correction. There is no universal experience; there is no universal women's experience. Leonard's primary concern in this article is on feminist experience, but she also illustrates how her Canadian experience differs from the U.S. experience.

American Catholic experience and theology

The theme of the 1971 convention, the first year of the second twenty-five years of the CTSA, was "The Impact of American Culture and Experience on Theology." The theme well illustrates the reality of historical consciousness. There is a place and even a need for an American theology. John H. Wright of the Jesuit theologate in Berkeley in his keynote address explicitly dealt with our topic, "The Meaning and Characteristics of an American Theology." Some might question the validity of the very idea of an American theology. The notion of a single ideal theology is most attractive, but there has never been such a theology that is not marked by the history and culture of the time and place in which it was developed. A distinctly American theology does not want to isolate the American experience as the only theology, but to draw on the American experience and wisdom to contribute to the whole of theology. History reminds us that we have always had such historical and temporal realities occasioning different approaches to theology. Peculiar dimensions of religion of all types in American life include pluralism, voluntarism, Pietism, and a certain involvement in the secular.

Wright then develops action characteristics of American life, including the blessing of God on the American experience and the emphasis on freedom, but also what Wright calls "the original sin" or the negative aspect of the American situation before God, especially institutional injustices with regard to others such as Native Americans and the slavery of Black people. Wright thus is not uncritical about the American experience but recognizes both its positive and negative aspects. Theology should strive to interpret American religious experience in terms of American values or operational categories, such as freedom, peace, justice, and love. The life communicated to us by the Holy Spirit will flourish as our decisions move us toward justice, peace, equality, and a society of free people. Wright is content with justifying the need for an American theology and pointing out these general parameters of this development (1971, 18–32).

The response of David Tracy from the University of Chicago to Wright's paper agrees that "the problem of historical consciousness is *the* problem which any contemporary theology must eventually face" (1971, 34). He agrees with the need for a cultural theology but cautions that these different cultural theologies can also show that religious, philosophical, and theological meanings involve an authentically transformational discussion. This is the task of fundamental theology (1971, 23–32).

In keeping with the theme of the 1971 convention, Christopher Mooney's "Christology in the Contemporary American Experience" maintains that the principal task of Christology today is to uncover those dimensions of human experience in which talk about Christ is meaningful. The Scriptures cannot totally satisfy our questions today since they were directed to people who had different cultures and experiences. The basic question is this: How is faith in Christ to function and be expressed in contemporary culture without being identified with those cultures?

Mooney describes the upheaval in American culture at this time as involving the dissatisfaction of youth, the protests of the Black community, resistance to the Vietnam War, and alarm over ecological devastation. What is being experienced in these different manifestations is the threat of the impersonal against the personal. Any new experience of transcendental meaning for Christ today must reflect that of the New Testament Christ who promises and accomplishes something new, justifies sinners, unsettles the self-satisfied, and guarantees a future to the oppressed. The Christ experience in the upheavals of our contemporary American culture is hope, which links the present to the historical Jesus and to the future fulfillment of his promises (1971, 38–55).

Three of the many papers at the 1971 convention deal with the distinctive American contribution to liturgy, the Church, and religious life. In his 1971 paper, "Is There a Distinct American Contribution to the Development of the Liturgy?," Godfrey Diekmann recognizes that liturgical development in America was derivative from Europe. The American experience can claim, however, four interpretations of liturgical reform that had some influence on Vatican II and continue to be important. He first mentions liturgy seen in relationship to social reform, which in my judgment may have been the most important contribution. The most significant person in the development of liturgical reform in the United States was the Collegeville Benedictine Virgil Michel. He founded in 1926 the journal *Orate Fratres*, which later changed its name to *Worship*, and was also involved in starting Liturgical Press. Michel, however, was neither a theologian nor a trained liturgist. In his academic life, he taught philosophy, but his consuming life interest was social justice. Thus, he brought to liturgical reform the important relationship between liturgy and social reform and justice. He encouraged two of his friends to publish *Liturgy and Sociology* in 1936. The journal lasted only two years, but it illustrates his pioneering contribution to liturgical renewal. For too long, liturgy was viewed one-sidedly as the public worship of God and social reform separately as action in the world. Diekmann honestly and humbly admits that, as the second editor of *Orate Fratres*, he had the willingness but not the genius of Virgil Michel to carry out this linkage of liturgy and social reform.

The other three distinctive characteristics of the liturgical reform in the United States insist on seeing liturgical reform in relation to other important dimensions and not merely as one isolated aspect. Efforts were made to bring liturgical renewal and catechetics together. The national liturgical weeks in the United States by the late 1950s and early 1960s attracted leaders from all other apostolates and renewal groups in the country. I recall how pleased I was to be asked to address the 1965 Liturgical Week in Chicago on the reform of moral theology. Another example of this pioneering attempt was to bring Church law in support of liturgical renewal as illustrated in the writings of Frederick McManus. As for the future, Diekmann hopes that the United States will be able to play a significant role in carrying out liturgical experimentation as set out in paragraphs 37–40 of the Constitution on the Liturgy. He ends his paper with a realistic observation that we have the opportunity and responsibility to carry out well-developed liturgical experimentation. All that is necessary is to convince the powers that be (1971, 200–210).

Richard McBrien's "Is There a Distinct American Contribution to the Notion of Church?" recognizes freedom as the most distinctive American contribution to a theology of the Church but cautions that freedom does not constitute the whole of ecclesiology. Those who do ecclesiology in the United States must emphasize freedom and consequently defend the separation and limitation of powers both of the state and in the Church. American ecclesiologists thus should support reforms that make the principle of the consent of the governed prevalent in every aspect of Church life and mission—whether in the formation of parish and diocesan councils, the widening of the process of the selection of bishops, the introduction of due process, and the revision of Canon Law. If the Church is to be a credible sign of God's reign in our country, it must be a kingdom of freedom, as well as a kingdom of truth, justice, and peace (1971, 211–25).

Luke Salm of Manhattan College, in his address "Is There a Distinct American Contribution to the Future of Religious Life?," recognizes that before Vatican II, for the most part, Catholics with just a few adjustments accepted the model of religious life developed in Europe. Salm briefly discusses four challenges for the future of religious life, which in one sense are universal but which pertain to American culture and experience—radicalism, pluralism, permanence, and secularism. Radicalism as proposed by Salm wants to forget the past and start anew from scratch, while traditionalism wants to hold on to the past. Salm favors a renewalist approach, which wants to find a middle way, but the problem is very real. Gone are the days of a uniform schedule, corporate commitment, and homogeneity of thought, spirit, and style in religious life. How to balance pluralism and homogeneity is a huge challenge. There is also much discussion about permanence and the possibility of temporary vows. Secularization poses a fundamental challenge to the notions of mission and prayer. These four challenges both threaten the future existence of religious life and offer the greatest hope for the future. He notes that his paper and others won't solve the problems, but religious themselves, theologians, and the whole Catholic community must become engaged in dealing with these challenges.

Liberation theologies

A third example of historical consciousness is liberation theology in its many different forms. This theology begins with the experience of the oppressed and the poor. Gustavo Gutiérrez, the father of liberation theology, gave papers at two meetings of the CTSA in the twenty-five-year time frame from 1971 to 1995. In the 1978 convention with the theme of "Voices in the Church," Gutiérrez addressed "The Voice of the Poor in the Church" (1978, 30–34). The paper begins by raising the question if it is possible to continue doing theology today in the dire situation of the poor in Latin America. His answer is yes, precisely because the voice of the poor must be heard. Liberation theology is a second act—reflection on praxis. This method is not simply a technological theological approach. It requires a spirituality involving living with the poor. In this context of oppression and death of the poor, the struggle for liberation is truly the struggle for life. Liberation theologies are not primarily concerned with some future society but are concerned about the nonnecessity of the present situation of the poor. Perhaps there is need for diverse voices in dialogue in the Church, but for the moment he prefers "voices in confrontation" (1978, 34).

At the 1992 convention with the theme of "Experience and Theology: A Critical Approximation?" Gutiérrez gave a plenary address: "Theology from the Experience of the Poor" (1992, 26–33). A word of caution is necessary here. The text as found in the *Proceedings* is a transcription from the talk that he gave. Gutiérrez emphasizes again the coherence between orthodoxy and orthopraxy, the experience of the poor as theological method, and the experience of the poor as the way to God. Gutiérrez here insists that a preferential option for the poor should challenge all Christians and all theologies, but living with the poor is only one source of reflection. We must be aware of the complexity of theological sources. Gutiérrez here recognizes the complexity and pluralism of theologies.

At the 1977 convention, Gregory Baum of St. Michael's in Toronto, Canada, with his expertise in theology and sociology, critically addressed the hermeneutic circle of the liberation theologian Juan Segundo. Segundo's hermeneutic circle goes through four steps: (1) it begins with a new experience that shatters the theologian's worldview; (2) the suspicion arises that the distortion shattered in the first phase has affected the understanding of Scripture itself; (3) this positive phase recognizes that Scripture and tradition contain elements agreeing with the shattering experience; (4) the fourth phase is a reinterpretation of the Church's tradition in light of the critical biblical discovery.

Baum's primary difficulty comes from the first phase of the shattering experience. History shows that the shattering experience in the past has sometimes led to both racist and fascist approaches. Thus, one needs in the first place to subject the shattering experience to biblical criticism so that the shattering experience truly leads to what is true and good. In addition, there are many shattering experiences, such as feminist theology, Black theology, and even Hispanic theology. Thus, Baum points out that even among people dedicated to world justice, there is a variety of different possible approaches.

Feminist theology, which began with the experience of the oppression from patriarchy and sexism, is another form of liberation theology that came to the fore, especially in the United States. What appears to be the first plenary address dealing with feminism as such was the paper of Mary J. Buckley of St. John's in New York at the 1979 CTSA convention, "Rising of the Woman in the Rising of the Race." Her method begins with the experience of women with regard to patriarchy and sexism and insight from the social sciences. As her title indicates, she sees the rising of women connected to the rising of the race and freedom from all forms of oppression. In discussing three anthropological models for women, she rejects the dual-nature model and the one-nature model and supports a transformative personal model, which also calls for transforming the social and cultural structures of our world. Such an approach calls for overcoming the gender and subordinate roles of women in personal and public life. The so-called feminine virtues of patience, support, caring, and so forth are virtues for all and not just for women. A truly transformed society overcoming the realities of sexism, racism, and classism is in some ways a utopia. The Christian faith vision, however, with its reign of justice and peace gives one the strength and courage to work for such a utopian vision—women and men who are full human subjects in a transformed culture and supported by Gospel values (1979, 48–63).

A year earlier in 1978, Buckley's paper "Rediscovering God: A Feminist Perspective" argues that male dominance is a system of injustice and oppression. To use core images for God that entrench this injustice is ultimately idolatry. In this paper, as well as the previous one, Buckley appeals to both sexual and racial liberation for a more adequate and truly Christian understanding of God (1978, 148–54). In both papers, Buckley frequently cites Rosemary Radford Ruether, who is often referred to as the mother of feminist theology in this·country. Ruether, however, at this time was not that active in the life of the CTSA. She did participate in the 1979 convention in a forum with Gregory Baum and Alfred Hennelly on "Theology and the Social Sciences: The Issues at Puebla." Ruether laments the lack of feminist liberation perspectives in the documents coming from the Latin American bishops at Puebla. The only significant discussion is the Commission on the Laity's document, which speaks of the oppression and exploitation of women in many areas (1979, 176–82). The comparatively small contribution of Ruether is a good reminder that Catholic theology is much broader and deeper than what is found in the comparatively small number of papers delivered in the history of the CTSA conventions.

Lisa Sowle Cahill's 1993 presidential address was the first presidential address to specifically discuss feminism—"Feminist Ethics and the Challenges of Cultures." Cahill insists that feminism as she understands it is inherently particular in its origins but is universal in its agenda. It seeks to be transformational in changing the oppression of women. Feminists can and should judge certain practices, institutions, and acts as wrong and can and should work to improve women's situations across cultures in matters such as self-determination, health, and education.

To hold onto the importance of particularity and the need for what I call a chastened universality, Cahill brings together her feminism as well as the best of the Aristotelian-Thomistic moral approach. Cahill strongly opposes the contemporary Catholic hierarchical understanding of natural law as found in the teachings on human sexuality. Such an approach to natural law is not the best of the Aristotelian-Thomistic tradition. Cahill also opposes the relativism of much of postmodern thinking. Aristotelian-Thomism at its best is inductive and thus provides a way to ground truth claims in a culturally mediated but reliable stratum of common human experience to address the many injustices in our world (1992, 65–83).

Another group that has suffered poverty and oppression is the Hispanic Catholic community in the United States. Virgilio Elizondo, rightly described as the father of Hispanic theology in the United States, gave three papers at CTSA conventions in 1975 (163–76), 1981 (155–70), and 1993 (1–14). The 1975 paper was part of the challenge to theology coming from the marginalized groups—women, Hispanics, and Blacks. Elizondo points out that even in 1975 Hispanic Catholics constituted 30 percent of the U.S. Catholic Church. Hispanic Catholics are people who have been twice conquered, twice colonized, and twice oppressed. The first conquest came at the hands of the Spanish conquistadores, who claimed to bring the Gospel to the native people of this area but, in reality, oppressed them and used them for their own purposes. The second wave of conquest and oppression came from U.S. white Catholics who came into the U.S. Southwest and looked down on the poor, uneducated Hispanics with their popular piety, which was so different from that of the white Church. The white Catholic population in the United States had a bureaucratic, rationalistic, and legalistic understanding of Church. White U.S. Catholics looked down on Mexican Catholics. U.S. Hispanic people did not become priests and religious because it meant estrangement from their community and culture. Elizondo appeals for a Catholic Church that is truly catholic and all-embracing, where the white Church can learn from the Hispanic Church and the Hispanic Church can learn from the white Church. Some progress has been made in these directions. Elizondo points to the Academy of Catholic Hispanic

Theologians in the United States (ACHTUS), which began in the late 1980s and started publishing in 1993 a peer-reviewed journal—the *Journal of Hispanic/Latino Theology*.

In 1987 and 1988, Orlando Espín and Sixto Garcia from the seminary at Boynton Beach in Florida did a workshop on Hispanic American theology and maintain that popular religiosity is a unique hermeneutical entity for developing Hispanic theology. They recognize four sources of moral theology—Scripture, tradition, liturgy, and human experience, with special emphasis on tradition. Popular religious piety is a legitimate form of tradition and not just a bastardized form of mainstream tradition in need of "purification" (i.e., assimilation into European and North American understandings of tradition). There is historical evidence that the dogmas of today emerged from popular belief, piety, and liturgies. They show how popular religious forms of tradition can affect various aspects of Catholic theology. Such an approach to Hispanic American theology is both an important part of a truly Hispanic Church theology in the service of the whole Church in this country and a prophetic challenge to those situations of injustice, disgrace, and nonmeaning imposed on Hispanic American Catholics through neglect, discrimination, and even overt contempt (1987, 114–19; 1988, 122–25).

As mentioned earlier, Joseph Nearon, the only Black member of the CTSA for many years, was appointed as head of the Research Committee for Black Theology and gave a long paper at the 1975 convention (1975, 173–202). Here he summarizes the literature of non-Catholic Black theology in this country. Many Black people look on the Catholic Church as a white man's church. Black people find it extremely difficult to be at home in the Catholic community. White Catholics are part of the dominant racist society in the United States. (There were only three Black bishops in the U.S. Catholic Church at that time.) The U.S. emphasis on the melting pot makes it even more difficult to recognize the reality of the role of Black Catholics in the Church. There is the need for liberation. Reconciliation can occur only after liberation. Racism is a social sin. His paper is just the beginning. There is need for a core of Black Catholic theologians to carry out this work of Black liberation.

In the 1980s and early 1990s, a small group of Black Catholic women carried out this work. In a 1982 panel on "Women and Power in the Church," Jaime Phelps, at that time a doctoral student at the Catholic University of America, pointed out that Black Catholics within the Church are extremely marginalized and because of their comparatively small number have no real influence. Black Catholics today are certain that the Church will not be firmly rooted in the Black tradition until there are many more Black ministers of salvation in the Church (1982, 119–23). In 1989, discussing providence, Phelps insists on a Black liberationist understanding of providence, calling Christians to participate in the liberation of Black Americans from the oppression of racism and all its institutionalized social, economic, and political forms (1989, 12–18). In response to a paper on Christology at the 1994 convention (1994, 147–55), Phelps formulates her question: How is Jesus the answer to the existential, familial, and communitarian questions of women who are subject to the triple oppression of race, gender, and class, particularly Black women? She then develops a recapitulation of Christology from a womanist perspective.

In a plenary panel at the 1991 convention, M. Shawn Copeland's "Theology as Intellectually Vital Inquiry: A Black Theological Interpretation" appeals to both Black theology and the thought of Bernard Lonergan to put forward a critical mediation of the Christian Gospel that takes into full account racism, sexism, classism, exploitation, and human objectification in a capitalistic system of production (1991, 41–57). Copeland would continue to explore this proposal in the third twenty-five-year period of the CTSA.

Fundamental Theology

This section will discuss the significant role of fundamental theology in the time frame between 1971 and 1995 in the *Proceedings* of the CTSA. Fundamental (or foundational) theology is generally understood in the Catholic tradition as the starting point for the various disciplines within Catholic theology. It provides the solid foundations for the work of the entire terrain of all particular theological aspects, such as historical, philosophical, systematic, moral, sacramental, and spiritual. This section will discuss the influential role of Karl Rahner, Bernard Lonergan, and David Tracy in the papers given at the CTSA between 1971 and 1995.

The German Jesuit Karl Rahner was without doubt the most significant Catholic theologian in the Vatican II and post–Vatican II period. The theme of the 1984 convention of the CTSA was "The World Church." This theme was taken from Rahner, who maintained that the main achievement of Vatican II was to have been the first official self-actualization of Catholicism as a world Church.[16] The theme and papers at the 1984 convention were developed in the year preceding the convention itself. However, Rahner himself died on March 30, 1984. Michael Fahey was to give the presidential address that year. He had been thinking of comparing Catholic theology in the years 1904 and 1984, since 1904 was the year of birth for John Courtney Murray, Yves Congar, Bernard Lonergan, and Karl Rahner. After hearing of Rahner's death, he changed his topic — "Presidential Address: 1904–1984, Karl Rahner, Theologian" (1984, 84–98). Fahey's paper includes sections on Rahner's conflicts with Church authority, the genesis and scope of his publications, and the influence he had on the CTSA. Rahner is not cited in any papers given in the first ten years of the CTSA, 1946–56. It was only in 1963 that the influence of Rahner began to be felt in the CTSA. Part of the reason was that English translations of Rahner's voluminous writings were comparatively late. In fact, as Fahey points out, some important works were not even translated by 1984. The first volumes of *Theological Investigations* (his collection of essays) were only published in English in 1961, whereas Rahner began the series in 1954. Fahey points out that of Rahner's forty-three doctoral students, five were members of the CTSA, and other members of the CTSA attended his lectures. This helps to explain how in the 1960s Rahner came to have a greater influence in the role of the CTSA even though his works were not all translated.

In 1991, another generation of CTSA members started the Karl Rahner Society, which has met at the CTSA meetings ever since. Seventy theologians were present at the first meeting. The purposes of this society are to study Rahner and to continue the Rahnerian enterprise by studying his thought and bringing him into dialogue with ongoing issues in theology and philosophy (1991, "The Karl Rahner Society," appendix C). The 1992 meeting of the Rahner Society, in keeping with the theme of the convention, "Theology as Intellectually Vital Inquiry," discussed three papers on nature, grace, and experience; Rahner on the human experience of God; and the experience of grace in relation to Rahner's philosophy of the heart (1992, 84–86). There is now in the CTSA a large institutional representation of people interested in the ongoing Rahner enterprise.

In his 1980 discussion of "Orthopraxis and Theological Method: Rahner," Leo O'Donovan, who wrote his dissertation under Rahner, develops his paper in light of the discussion especially in Europe that sees Rahner as using a transcendental method that is insensitive to social problems and ineffectual in the realm of political or social change. A footnote identifies this approach with the well-known position of Johann Baptist Metz. Today, the question is not so much how we can know God, but rather how self-serving images of God can be shattered and replaced by images that call for a more just society. These approaches contend that Rahner gives primacy to theory that minimizes the social and political aspect and the need for orthopraxis. In this paper, O'Donovan maintains that Rahner's approach does recognize the political and social and the need for orthopraxis. He develops his thesis in four steps. First, Rahner has emphasized that to approach a theological question adequately, one must approach it from both a transcendental and a historical perspective. The method is twofold whose movements are dialectically related. In his approach to method, anthropology, grace, Christology, and Trinity, Rahner has repeatedly argued for this reciprocal interdependence of transcendental and historical reflection in theology. However, O'Donovan does recognize the need for a more explicit development of this historical moment in Rahner's method.

Second, another misconception maintains Rahner's method is anthropological in an exclusive sense. But Rahner has consistently sought to root the grace of God in human experience, recalling often that unless we appreciate the scope of the human, we cannot appreciate how God's own life may be its innermost origin and ultimate good. Another way of phrasing the objection that Rahner is too exclusively anthropological is that his method leaves out the conflictual and negativity in life, such as the horrors of the Holocaust or Hiroshima or the poverty of the Third World. On the contrary, O'Donovan insists that Rahner's anthropology is inclusive, containing the seeds of the very objections brought against him. The third step challenges the misrepresentation that Rahner's is a theological method erected on a philosophical foundation. O'Donovan insists that it is a thoroughly theological method. His theology is centered in the current uniqueness of living faith. This has led him both to the lecture platform and to the pulpit to make faith incarnate now. Spiritual experience leads to existential decision.

In the fourth step, O'Donovan portrays what for Rahner is the whole science. Theology is a way of leading the Christian community deeper into the true mystery of its life. It is a science of the mystery. In the divine mystery, theology finds that we are for God and for one another—a dialectic of truth and love. Christian reflection, however critical, and Christian love, however committed, must always involve a surrender to the mystery of God, a final trust and adoration, a silence that is faith.

As O'Donovan points out, Rahner was always reluctant to talk about the method of his theology. In this article, he shows that Rahner's approach is more than transcendental, anthropological, and philosophical, thus refuting some of the criticisms that have been raised against Rahner's approach as not giving enough importance to the political and social. Francis Fiorenza, then at Villanova University, a practical theologian who was a student of both Rahner and Metz, in his 1977 paper, "Political Theology as Fundamental Theology," recognizes that the political dimension of theology is not the exclusive horizon for understanding Christian doctrine. There are also existential and transcendental horizons (1977, 146).

Bernard Lonergan was an early member of the CTSA and is the only person who was awarded both the Cardinal Spellman Award (1949) and the John Courtney Murray Award (1973). His own writings and those of his students and others have made an enormous contribution to Catholic theology. There are seven Lonergan institutes or centers in North America, as well as others outside that area. The Lonergan Institute at Boston College provides Lonergan studies both inside and outside Boston College itself. The week-long Lonergan Workshop began in the early

1970s and continues to exist. The Lonergan Research Institute at Regis College in Toronto houses all of Lonergan's papers. Its library has an exhaustive collection of primary and secondary literature on Lonergan. Since 1980, it has published a *Lonergan Studies Newsletter*. Its most important project is the projected publication of twenty-five volumes in the series of Collected Works of Bernard Lonergan.[17] Bernard Lonergan is far and away the most outstanding North American theologian in the post–Vatican II period.

The previous section used Lonergan's notion of historical consciousness to display the various types of theology that begin from a particular starting point. The most significant paper Lonergan gave at the CTSA was his 1972 "The Revolution of Theology" because it gave indications about his method (1972, 18–23). That same year, he published *Method in Theology*, which is totally devoted to developing this method. His article provides hints and parameters about his method.[18] Despite the fact that he does not develop the concept of historical consciousness in this article, such a reality plays a significant role. In the past, culture was considered normatively and, accordingly, there was just one culture for all humankind. But we now have an empirical notion of culture because culture is simply the set of meanings and values that inform the way of life of the community. Cultures are many and varied. Culture affects the historicity of the person. It is the historically existing culture that provides the matrix within which persons live and develop. The mission of the Church is to proclaim the gospel, but today it must insert the gospel into a new and different culture and not impose what was previously thought to be the one and only culture. The shift from a normative to an empirical culture recognizes that one can no longer think of the Church as a perfect society but rather as an ongoing process of self-realization. In addition, the ancient Greeks did not grasp contemporary notions of science and philosophy. Physicists used to talk about the necessary laws of nature, but now they speak of the statistical possibilities of quantum theory. The outlook of modern scientific doctrine is not an intelligibility that is necessary but an intelligibility that is possible and probably verified. This shift from an intelligibility that is a necessity to the intelligibility that is a possibility and, as well, probably verified calls for the dethronement of the speculative intellect or pure reason. The philosopher does not begin with the necessary and self-evident truths. The sciences, including theology, in the future will be rooted in the cognitional and psychological operations of the knowing and loving person. This approach puts emphasis on the different types of conversion and the role of deliberating, evaluating, deciding, and loving. For a good summary of Lonergan's paper, see the response of Austin Vaughan (1972, 24). This revolution in theology is comparable to the revolution of theology in the twelfth and thirteenth centuries. What Lonergan is proposing is a new method for theology.

The third fundamental theologian to be considered is David Tracy, who has spent most of his career at the University of Chicago. Tracy was a graduate student of Lonergan's but has developed in his own way. Earlier, we mentioned Tracy's insistence on the importance of fundamental theology. This section will concentrate on his presidential address in 1977, "The Catholic Analogical Imagination" (1977, 234–44). Tracy claims that within the vibrant pluralism and strong disagreements among Catholic theologians at this time, there exists an element of shared vision, which he calls the analogical imagination. He uses the word *imagination* to describe the horizon prior to our explicit beliefs of the meaning of the whole more theologically. When we use our imagination creatively, we do not simply report on the reality we ordinarily see in our everyday life. Rather, when we imagine, especially when we imagine the reality inspired by God's gift of faith and revelation, we redescribe the creative possibilities of all reality. There is, thus, this common vision that all Catholic theologians despite all their diversity bring to their theological enterprise.

Tracy uses the phrase "analogical imagination" to refer to the horizon that defines the uniqueness of Catholic theology. The analogical imagination is distinguished from the dialectical relationship. For the analogical imagination, there is some order to be found in reality, and the key to that order will be found in some focal meaning, which focuses on the basic clue to the whole and by means of that clue envisions all our multiple relationships. For Catholics, that clue, that focal meaning, is the incarnation that tells us who God is; who we are; how the cosmos itself is a sacrament of God's love; how ordered community is possible; how reason can be trusted; and how the final reality is neither error, nor illusion, nor death, nor sin, but a radical nonsentimentalized love as the final key to the order and transcendence of all reality. For the dialectical imagination, there is no hope for such order. The authentic person's task is to unmask illusions and idolatries and to be suspicious of all claims to a vision of the whole. The analogical imagination avoids the extremes of total skepticism about some order and monism that embraces only order. The analogical imagination both appropriates and transforms the genuine insights of the dialectical mind. Tracy then shows the presence of the analogical imagination in the language of Catholic theology and in Catholic themes of social justice. Tracy illustrates how this analogical imagination is found in the patristic writers, the medieval theologians, Thomistic and neo-Thomistic theologies, and transcendental Thomists, as well as in liberation and political theologians. A curiously overlooked passage in Vatican I states that theology is the partial, incomplete, analogous, but real understandings of the mysteries of the Catholic faith. Note here the presence of the analogical imagination. Political and liberation theologians incorporate more explicitly dialectical modes of reflection in their model, but they are eventually transformed into the Catholic analogical context. Despite all the illusion, distortions, error, stupidity, and sin, grace endures and finally prevails. This analogical imagination acknowledges the final trustworthiness of all reality embraced by the love of God and is the genius of the vision of Catholic Christianity.

This final section has discussed the importance of Karl Rahner, Bernard Lonergan, and David Tracy in the ongoing life of the CTSA at this time with the important role of fundamental or foundational theology. In my judgment, the three areas of the tension between Church authority and theology, the various implications of historicity and historical consciousness, and the important role of fundamental theology are three very significant aspects of the theology found in the papers of the CTSA in its second twenty-five years of existence.

Chapter 4

THE CATHOLIC THEOLOGICAL SOCIETY OF AMERICA, 1996–2020

There were significant differences and discontinuities between the first twenty-five years of the CTSA and the second twenty-five years. The differences between the second twenty-five years and the third twenty-five years exist, but they are not as dramatic as between the first two time frames. This chapter will first consider the internal life of the CTSA at this time and then the theological content of the papers.

INTERNAL LIFE

In many ways, the internal life of the CTSA built on and consolidated what had been developed in the second twenty-five-year time frame. Perhaps the most significant change concerned the sponsored research projects that were present after 1970. For all practical purposes, these did not continue to exist after 1996. One can only speculate on what caused this quite dramatic change. Perhaps there was no felt need for such research projects sponsored by the CTSA. The growing publications of members were dealing with the issues raised for theology. Perhaps there no longer was the financial resource for the projects coming from the bishops. Without doubt the problems and controversies surrounding some research reports, such as *Human Sexuality*, contributed to the feeling there was no longer a place for such sponsored research projects.

Members

The number of members grew but not all that much. The reason for the growth spurt in the second period was the growth of the academic nature of theology taught in Catholic higher education and the number of universities now giving doctoral degrees. A good illustration of the lack of a growth spurt in the number of members in this time frame comes from the number of members attending meetings. As already mentioned, the fiftieth anniversary meeting in New York attracted 535 members. According to the statistics released at the annual meetings, that was the highest number ever to attend a CTSA convention. For example, the seventy-fourth convention in Pittsburgh in 2019 had 422 members attending. The lowest number of attendees during this twenty-five-year period was the 340 members who attended the 2009 convention in Halifax, Nova Scotia. The cost of transportation to this place far distant from the areas where members taught and lived contributed to this low number. The meetings in Toronto and Ottawa, for example, have not shown such a decline in attendance.

Regarding membership, one important change was the introduction of a graduated dues structure at the 2004 convention (2004, 194). In 2003, the membership was polled and 82 percent were in favor of this change, replacing the older, fixed amount of dues for everyone. One could make the case that Catholic social teaching, with its emphasis on the fact that those who have more should contribute more in dues for the common good, strongly supports such a change. The dues for 2005 were fixed as follows:

Less than $20,000 — $30
$20,000–$30,000 — $60
$30,000–$40,000 — $75
$40,000–$50,000 — $90
$50,000–$60,000 — $105
More than $60,000 — $120

The present dues structure is:

Less than $20,000 — $40
$20,000–$30,000 — $70
$30,000–$40,000 — $85
$40,000–$50,000 — $100
$50,000–$60,000 — $115
Over $60,000 — $130

Based on Catholic social ethics and teaching, one could maintain that one or two higher categories should exist, because some university professors have larger salaries. Nevertheless, the change in the dues structure enabled the society to support several important projects that will be mentioned later.

An effort was made to attract and support new members. Throughout the twenty-five-year period, the practice continued having a presidential reception for new and newer members after the business meeting on Friday in the early evening. In 2004, the CTSA initiated the CTSA Best Article Award by new scholars. Board member and future president María Pilar Aquino had developed this proposal, and the board readily accepted it. Applicants should be active or associate members of the CTSA who are doctoral students in theological programs or nontenured professors whose doctorate was conferred less than three years prior to the submission of the article. The author whose essay is thus recognized will receive a plaque of recognition and an honorarium of $500 (2004, 192). In 2005, the first winner of the Award for Best Academic Essay by a Young Scholar was Gemma Tulude Cruz from Radboud University, Nijmegen in the Netherlands for her essay "One Bread, One Body, One People: The Challenge of Migration to Theological Reflection." An abstract of the paper was given in the *Proceedings* (2005, 179–80). At the 2006 meeting, the Best Essay Award was renamed in honor of Catherine Mowery LaCugna, whose recent and premature death affected many. That year, the award was given to Laura M. Taylor of Vanderbilt University (2006, 204). The award has been given annually at the end of the business meeting on Friday afternoon ever since. Also, at the 2006 meeting the president-elect reported an innovation— "breakfast with a new member." Fourteen new members and twice that number of CTSA members signed up. The intention was that these breakfasts would continue.

At the 2010 meeting, the president reported that the board voted to contribute $12,000 annually, depending on the market, to defray convention costs for graduate students and junior scholars. The board refined eligibility requirements and prepared an application form. Senior members were asked to make this opportunity known to junior colleagues and graduate students (2010, 193). The 2011 presidential report elaborated on this proposal of grants up to $1,000 for graduate students, junior scholars, and members who are presently unemployed or whose institutions do not provide the funding for attending the convention (2011, 199). At the 2019 meeting, the president-elect hosted a "mentorship breakfast" with the theme "Navigating as a Newcomer." About thirty members attended, primarily newer, younger members. If evidence indicates this initiative is helpful, it will be done again in the future.

Thus, in this twenty-five-year space, significant efforts to support the attendance and participation of new and younger members in the conventions were made. The society is willing to use some of the surplus money to support such a worthy endeavor.

One of my concerns as a senior participant observer at this time was the attendance by the more senior and well-known members of the society. I wish the number of such attendees were more, but I am grateful for the many former presidents, award winners, and well-known senior members who have continued to come to the conventions. Some of these come to support their graduate students who are now presenting papers. Some come because one way or another they are connected with something on the program. Other such members come because they have a commitment for the good of the CTSA itself. The CTSA needs both the junior and senior members actively involved in the life of the society. On the whole, it seems to me that this balance has been achieved. It is important, however, for the CTSA itself to recognize the important role that senior members can and should play in the ongoing convention life of the society.

In the second twenty-five years of the story of the CTSA, especially at the beginning, women were an evident minority in the society. As this time frame developed, as mentioned in the last chapter, the number of women involved in the life of the CTSA increased dramatically for the reasons mentioned. By the beginning of the third twenty-five-year period of the life of the CTSA, women were no longer recognized as a minority. The Committee on Underrepresented Ethnic and Racial Groups that came into existence before the turn of the century recognized that the existing minority groups were primarily ethnic and racial. Statistics bear out this judgment.

The Women's Seminar has met every year during the twenty-five-year time frame on the Thursday afternoon before the "official" opening of the convention in the early evening. The Women's Seminar is now officially called the "Women's Consultation in Constructive Theology." In 1998, it began awarding the Anne O'Hara Graff Award to a woman member of the CTSA. The award honors the life and scholarly achievements of Anne O'Hara Graff who tragically died at the age of forty-six in 1996. The award is given to one who is outstanding in scholarship and the mentoring of women in the field. The award criteria tried to find a balance between senior and mid-career scholars, well-known and lesser-known scholars who still have made substantial contributions. The first recipient in 1998 was Joan Timmerman of the College of St. Catherine in St. Paul, Minnesota (2006, 222–23).

The number of women becoming new members was well over one-third of all the new members. In 2000, 28 percent were women (2000, 201); in 2006, 40 percent were women (2006, 199–200); in 2010, 39 percent were women (2010, 192); in 2015, about one-third were women (2015, 188). Women also had a growing number of the speaking roles at the conventions as the years went on. In 2010, 40 percent of the 117 speaking roles were women (2010, 184); in 2019, the women comprised 42 percent of the 130 speaking roles in the convention (2019, 206). In this twenty-five-year period, three women held the office of president in three of the first five years—Elizabeth Johnson (1996), Mary Ann Donovan (1998), and Margaret Farley (2000). Subsequent women presidents were M. Shawn Copeland (2004), Mary Catherine Hilkert (2006), Margaret O'Gara (2008), Mary Ann Hinsdale (2011), Susan A. Ross (2013), Susan K. Wood (2015), Mary Hines (2018), María Pilar Aquino (2020), and Christine Firer Hinze (2021). In the same twenty-five-year period, seven women received the John Courtney Murray Award—Anne E. Carr (1997), Agnes Cunningham (2001), Elizabeth Johnson (2004),

Sandra Schneiders (2006), Lisa Sowle Cahill (2008), Anne E. Patrick (2013), M. Shawn Copeland (2018). Thus, after seventy-five years, women are not only comfortable at the CTSA but also heavily involved in leadership roles.

In 1992, the first steps were taken by the board to improve the presence of underrepresented groups in the life of the CTSA (1992, 189). In 1998, the CTSA Committee for Underrepresented Ethnic and Racial Groups joined with four other organizations in sponsoring a recruitment conference to attract racial and ethnic minority students in religious studies and theology. The conference was scheduled to take place in September 1998 at Vanderbilt University (1998, 185). In 2001, the chair of the committee proposed a mentoring program for promising graduate students and new members (2001, 218). As time went on, this committee acquired the acronym CUERG and expanded its efforts. In 2005, CUERG defined its mission: "To recruit, mentor, and retain members of underrepresented groups and to promote awareness and engagement with theological scholarship." At a display table they showed examples of the scholarly work produced by members of these groups (2005, 179). At the same 2005 meeting, the president-elect reported that 4 percent of the names on the convention program were from underrepresented constituencies (2005, 178).

CUERG itself was growing and having more influence on the life of the society. At the 2007 meeting, CUERG reported on its activities to the business meeting—a practice that has been generally followed down to the present. Also at the 2007 meeting, CUERG hosted a luncheon for about thirty-five people, including students and recently graduated African, African American, Hispanic, and Asian Pacific scholars. The luncheon was paid for by the board and the Fund for Theological Education. Two Hispanic members raised the issue of the need for having more members from underrepresented groups as members of the CUERG (2007, 195).

The 2008 report to the convention pointed out that CTSA now has special sessions for Black, Latino/a, and Asian theology and for new members from underrepresented groups. Other groups, however, on the program are encouraged to have CUERG members on their programs, thus making them a part of the mainstream of the society (2008, 207–8). New members were encouraged to attend the CUERG luncheon on Saturday. A longer report on CUERG is found in appendix 2 of the 2008 convention. Among other things, the committee points out the danger of ghettoizing underrepresented groups apart from the broader society. In this connection, "mainstream" theologians are urged to incorporate the scholarly work of underrepresented groups in their teaching and writing in general and in their sessions at the CTSA (2008, 220–22). There is no need to record all that CUERG accomplished in the subsequent years. The board continued to support the work of CUERG and often gave some financial support to the annual luncheon at the convention.

CUERG's success is shown in the greater involvement of underrepresented groups as speakers at the convention. Remember that in 2005, 4 percent of the names on the program were from underrepresented groups, but in 2016, there were 123 members making presentations at the convention and forty-one of these came from underrepresented groups (2016, 163). Since 2000, five members from underrepresented groups have served as presidents of the CTSA—Peter Phan (2002), M. Shawn Copeland (2004), Roberto Goizueta (2005), Bryan Massingale (2010), María Pilar Aquino (2020). Since 2007, four members from underrepresented groups have received the John Courtney Murray Award—Virgilio Elizondo (2007), Peter Phan (2010), Orlando Espín (2016), and M. Shawn Copeland (2018).

An issue concerning the membership of the CTSA that has not been explicitly raised before is the fact that all Catholic theologians do not feel at home in the society. Chapter 3 mentioned that the Fellowship of Catholic Scholars came into existence in 1977, reacting against some of the activities of the CTSA. The first meeting of the Academy of Catholic Theologians took place in 2008. The mission statement asserts that the object of theology is given by revelation, interpreted in the Church under the authority of the magisterium, and received by faith.[1] These two groups strongly supported the noninfallible teachings of the hierarchical magisterium and opposed dissent. They obviously did not feel at home in the CTSA. The existence of these two societies pointed to some lack of diversity in the CTSA.

This issue would not come up for public discussion in the CTSA until Daniel Finn raised it in his 2007 presidential address, "Power and Public Presence in Catholic Social Thought, the Church, and the CTSA." His thesis in the third part of his address is that the public statements of the CTSA have caused the society problems. For all the good that the public statements have done, they have also caused us damage—and not because they were erroneous. These statements have become the public face of the CTSA for those who do not attend our meetings. These public statements present us as individuals who come together as a group primarily to defend ourselves against hierarchical authority. We insiders know this is only a small part of what we do. He admits that there are also serious problems with the work of the Congregation for the Doctrine of the Faith. If these public statements cause us to be misunderstood in the general public, we cannot ignore this representation and its effects. Finn recognizes that some have inadvertently or even malevolently misinterpreted what we do, but we cannot ignore the reality of the public perception of the CTSA.

The second reason why our public statements have caused us problems concerns the internal cost. There are many conservative theologians who used to attend the CTSA conventions who no longer do so. A good number are no longer even members. The

CTSA claims to be a forum for an exchange of views among Catholic theologians and with other scholars. The CTSA should be the place where Catholic theologians from all perspectives within the Church come to do theology. Finn admits that the price of achieving that dialogue is making fewer public statements to defend theologians against the ecclesiastical power. We are paying too high a price for the good that comes from such public statements. We have used the mechanics of democratic majority vote to undercut the mission of our society by producing statements that the minority will find offensive. Finn wishes we were not facing this trade off, but unfortunately, we are (2007, 73–75).

The CTSA itself has never publicly addressed the challenge laid down by Finn, but it has dealt with some aspects of it. I have occasionally mentioned that in telling the story of the CTSA my role is that of a participant observer. But in this issue, I am very much the participant. Not only have I strongly supported almost all the public statements of the CTSA, but probably no one has been the beneficiary of the CTSA's support more than I. *Caveat lector.* In an ideal world, I agree very much with the position that the CTSA should be the place where Catholic theologians from very different perspectives should come together to dialogue and debate. I have tried to facilitate such an all-encompassing approach in the twenty-volume series Readings in Moral Theology that I have edited and coedited. To be Catholic is to strive for inclusivity. But we do not live in an ideal world. There are divisions in the Church and divisions in Catholic theology. It is perhaps better to speak of differences, because all of us should recognize that we are united by our shared commitment to the good of the Church.

Our primary responsibility as theologians and as a theological society is to theologize to the best of our abilities. As the earlier chapters have shown, the role of theology in the post–Vatican II Church has changed. Theology no longer has the role of simply affirming what the magisterium teaches, but it should always respect the proper role of the magisterium in the Church.

Theology is in the service of the Church and is done for the good of the Church. Theology also has a public role since all in the Church have a right to know what theologians are saying. This is true not only for individual theologians but also for a society that says it is the largest theological society in the world. In the past, theologians have spoken out not just as individuals but also as theological faculties. Theological faculties in medieval times and later passed authoritative judgments on the orthodoxy of theological positions.[2] When groups such as faculties or societies speak out, the only way to determine what the society holds is by having a vote on the resolutions. The U.S. bishops themselves obviously vote on all issues, and there are many people who feel they are not represented by the statements of the conference itself. Yes, the CTSA has a responsibility to be conscious of its public image, but there can be and are other ways in which the society can show such a concern for all-inclusive approaches.

The thorny question of the relationship between theology and authority or theology and the magisterium will be discussed in greater detail later in this chapter. It is sufficient now to point out the issue should not be phrased in oppositional terms of authority versus theologians. The primary reality is truth. Both theology and the magisterium are seeking the truth. Inevitably, there will be some tensions between the two, but these differences must be seen in a mutual commitment to the good of the Church and the search for the truth.

In the context of Finn's comments, one should note that some more conservative theologians have remained members of the CTSA. A good example of this is the von Balthasar Society, which has generally scheduled a breakfast at the meetings of the CTSA in the last twenty-five years as well as a consultation. Also, in some of the disagreements with the CDF or the bishops, the public statements of the CTSA have simply pointed out that due process was not followed or even that the bishops did not follow the procedures they themselves accepted. Four plenary sessions in 2004, 2008, 2013, and 2014 were given by theologians who definitely disagreed with the majority of the members of the CTSA. At the 2016 convention, an invited group committed to dialogue among diverse theological positions was scheduled and followed by a three-year interest group dealing with the same topic. In 2017, Lisa Sowle Cahill and Nicholas J. Healy addressed the "liberal" and "conservative" approaches to sexuality. The convener of the session remarked that the atmosphere of the session with almost seventy persons was tense at times but always respectful—just what was wanted (2017, 137–38). The interest group on theological diversity at the 2018 convention had papers discussing the Church-world relationship from conservative and liberal positions. This interest group in 2019 had two papers on authority in the Church from these two different perspectives. Thus, the CTSA, perhaps with some prodding from Finn, has tried to make sure that diverse theological voices are heard at their conventions. But I still hold that for the good of theology, and especially for the good of the Church, it is sometimes necessary for the society to take public positions on controversial issues and actions that have been taken by the CDF and/or the bishops.

The Meetings

Throughout this period, Thursday afternoon before the official first session, the Women's Consultation on Constructive Theology met. Sometimes other preconvention sessions met on Thursday afternoon before the Women's Consultation. The opening session on Thursday evening included a welcome from the local bishop or his delegate followed by the first plenary speaker. The evening ended with a reception usually sponsored by some Catholic colleges and universities, often from the local area. Morning prayer took place on Friday and Saturday mornings. Three other plenaries and many breakout sessions took place on Friday and Saturday. The business meeting of the society was on late Friday afternoon. The business meeting began with the admission of the new members and the report of the nominating committee. The existing president-elect became the new president, and the vice president became the president-elect. The nominating committee proposed two names for vice president and four names for the two positions on the board of directors. There were seldom any nominations from the floor, probably because of the time commitment that each of these people had to be willing to make to serve the society. The past president also served on the board for one year. The secretary, treasurer, and executive director were demanding positions that had a longer term of office. The board appointed a nominating committee for these positions and presented one person for the position that the membership usually approved by acclamation. The president, other officers, as well as important committees made their reports to the members. If there were proposed resolutions, they were first of all accepted by the resolutions committee, discussed in an early afternoon session on Friday, and then presented at the end of the business meeting. Some resolutions, however, could be proposed at the business meeting with 25 percent of those attending agreeing to discuss such a resolution. As mentioned before, the LaCugna Award was announced at the business meeting and given to a junior scholar for the best essay ever since its inauguration in 2005 (2005, 179–80).

The convention eucharistic liturgy was usually held at a nearby church on late Saturday afternoon. If the president were a priest, he presided at the liturgy and gave the homily. If the president were not a priest, she or he appointed someone to preside at the liturgy, but the president gave the reflections at the liturgy. After the convention, the banquet was held. The banquet generally attracted about two-thirds of those attending the meeting. One of the problems here was the high cost for the banquet. At the end of the banquet, the president announced the winner of the John Courtney Murray Award who then responded. There was always some speculation among the members who would receive the Murray Award. One hint was that the awardee with her or his guests usually sat at two tables near the front. Then, finally, on Sunday morning, the presidential address was given.

The two biggest changes that occurred in this twenty-five-year period were the memorial for deceased members and the program on Sunday morning. In 2008, a memorial service was incorporated into the opening Thursday evening session (2008, 191). Before then, the recently deceased were mentioned at the business meeting or they were mentioned at the convention liturgy. This memorial service is quite moving and has continued to the present. The seventy-fifth-anniversary meeting in 2020 was cancelled because of the COVID-19 pandemic. In its place, however, there was a virtual meeting involving this memorial celebration. The memorial celebration included opening prayers and hymns followed by a one- or two-minute memorial for each person who died in the last year. After the individual memorial minute is given, the person giving the memorial lights a candle and places it on a table with all the other candles. After the memorial minutes are given, there are concluding prayers and a hymn.

The other change in the structure of the annual meeting concerns the Sunday morning session. The presidential address was always on Sunday morning in this time frame. Before 2005, there was another session before the presidential address starting at 9:00 a.m., with the presidential address at 11:00 a.m. and the brief appointment of the new president at noon. The first session had different formats, but in the years immediately before

2005, it had the form of "follow-up seminars," discussing in three different groups the three plenary sessions that had been given earlier (2004, 188–89). From 2005 on, however, the presidential address was scheduled from 9:00 a.m. to 10:00 a.m. with no discussion or question period, followed by the handing over of the gavel to the incoming president. Why the change? It seems many people were leaving early on Sunday and missing the presidential address, so it was the only event now scheduled on Sunday with the program ending at 10:00 a.m.

One aspect that was regularly mentioned in the CTSA meetings since 1996 is the involvement of the society with the International Network of Societies for Catholic Theology (INSeCT). At the 1996 meeting, the president reported the board's support for this project of global networking of all Catholic theology societies in the world. CTSA sent two delegates to the meeting in Sherbrooke, Canada, later that summer. The plan was for a meeting of the presidents of these groups or delegates to meet on a three-year cycle hosted by the European Society for Catholic Theology, the Conference of Catholic Theological Institutions (COCTI), and the CTSA (1996, 326). From its very beginning, INSeCT was a meeting of representatives and not a large meeting with many members present. The CTSA has financially supported this organization's work over the years as INSeCT itself developed. In 2016, an invited session at the CTSA convention contributed to INSeCT's global research project dealing with the role of women in decision-making in different areas of Church and society (2016, 66–67).

Every five years or so, the board revisited the structure of the convention program, especially dealing with the breakout sessions. In 2005, the president appointed a committee to study the issues. A proposed restructuring that made comparatively minor changes was proposed by the board to the 2006 meeting for a consultative vote (2006, 205–6). The slightly modified restructuring was approved in principle. In 2007, the president described the new structure beginning in 2008. There would be sixteen topic areas, seven consultations, and three interest groups. Topic areas and consultations would be ongoing. Interest groups would have a three-year term with no possibility of renewal. Each topic area (e.g., spirituality, Christology, bioethics) would have an administrative team of three members, with one member rotating off each year and a new member coming in. Each administrative team would have its own webpage where they could post "call for papers" and other notices. There would continue to be the presidential address, three plenary sessions, invited sessions, and selected sessions (2007, 192). In subsequent years, slight modifications were made in the structure of the meetings. Beginning in 2012, the *Proceedings* labeled the different types of sessions—plenary sessions, invited sessions, selected sessions (from those proposed by members), topic sessions, consultations, and interest groups. Such a structure allows for ongoing dialogue by members with regard to a topic session and consultation, while providing for one-time presentations in the invited and selected sessions. The 2019 format was basically the same.

The *Proceedings of the CTSA* have been published from the very first meeting in 1946. Two developments have occurred. First, in 2012, the *Proceedings* were published electronically and no longer in print (2011, 199–200). In the very beginning of the society, all the papers given at the convention were published in the *Proceedings*. As time went on and there were many more sessions in the program, not all of these could be printed in full. In the latter years, the general policy has been to publish in full the plenary papers with responses given if there were any responses and the presidential address. All the breakout sessions are summarized in a two-page summary of the papers that were given.

The Primary Tension

The primary tension in the internal life of the CTSA in the 1996 to 2020 time frame once again involves the relationship between Church authority and theology. *Ex corde Ecclesiae*, the 1990 apostolic constitution of Pope John Paul II, called for those teaching theological disciplines in Catholic higher education to have a mandate from the competent ecclesiastical authority, which is usually the local bishop. Since the promulgation of this document in 1990, the U.S. bishops have been considering their response to the application of *Ex corde* in the United States.

At the 1996 meeting, the president reported that the bishops' draft document for the implementation of *Ex corde* would be voted on by the bishops at their November meeting. The CTSA board was pleased because there was no mention of a mandate, and norms for resolving disputes would be those found in the Doctrinal Responsibilities based on the contributions of the CTSA and the CLSA (1996, 326). In 1997, the president asked Monika Hellwig of the Association of Catholic Colleges and Universities (ACCU) to update the society members on the Vatican's response to the bishops' implementation guidelines. Hellwig was the chair of the CTSA's own committee on *Ex corde* and the recipient of the John Courtney Murray Award in 1984. The ACCU also strongly opposed the call for a mandatum because it was seen as a violation of academic freedom and the autonomy of the university. The Vatican's response that the bishops' document was a "first draft" came as a surprise to the bishops. The bishops' implementation committee began proceeding slowly in formulating their new document. At the 1998 convention, Hellwig again reported. Bishop John Leibrecht was chair of the implementation committee of *Ex corde*, which was composed of both bishops and university presidents. A canonical subcommittee was working on the effects of the implementation and would respond to the full committee. In the 1999 convention, Hellwig reported on the discussions at the 1998 bishops' meeting on the implementation of *Ex corde*. The ACCU itself with help from the CTSA had written an alternative proposal and even met unofficially with some Vatican officials about it.

At the 2000 meeting, however, there was much discussion on this issue because the bishops in their fall 1999 meeting passed a new document that included the juridical legislation of Canon 812 calling for the mandate from ecclesiastical authority for all those teaching theological disciplines in Catholic higher education. One sees here again the pressure that the Vatican put on the U.S. bishops to change their position. A special session was held at the CTSA convention to discuss the document with its need for a mandate. President Margaret Farley noted that the CTSA had asked the bishops to speak with theologians before taking their vote in 1999, but they did not do so. The bishops, however, expressed a desire to dialogue with theologians about details of the implementation. The CTSA appointed a new committee chaired by John Boyle to address the issue of the mandatum. Bishop Joseph Fiorenza, the president of the bishops' conference, appointed a committee chair who would contact the CTSA and the CLSA for names of theologians to serve on a committee to work out the process for the mandatum. President Farley also announced that the CTSA would host and financially support regional meetings of chairs of departments of religious studies and theology with local bishops to facilitate dialogue about *Ex corde* and the mandatum and to explore the possibilities of having regular meetings with the local bishops. The board believed these meetings would have intrinsic value in themselves, and there were no plans to collect the information from these individual meetings (2000, 202–3).

The shoe had finally dropped. The mandate had been on the horizon for many years, but now it became a reality. One could maintain that the opposition of theologians in general and the CTSA in particular was simply a case of self-interest for theologians. There is some truth here, but the theological enterprise and its opposition to the mandate was based on what is good for the Church. Catholic colleges and universities opposed the mandate for the same reason. The reluctance of the U.S. bishops for a long time to support the mandate indicates that much more than theological self-interest was involved. The growing centralization of the Church under the papacy of John Paul II added to the fears that the mandate if strictly enforced would not be for the good of the Church, Catholic higher education, and the role of theology. There was great trepidation about the future.

The focus of all those involved centered on how the processes surrounding the mandate would function. As to be expected, the report about the mandate by the president at the 2001 meeting was long and detailed. The CTSA was in contact with the bishops' committee chaired by Archbishop Daniel Pilarczyk concerning implementation of the mandate, but the CTSA president was dissatisfied with the original consultation process used by the bishops' committee. The CTSA cooperated with the bishops' committee to promote local gatherings between bishops and theologians. Reports suggest that these meetings were cordial, modestly informative, and achieved some lessening of tensions, although some bishops did not really respond to the pertinent questions raised by the theologians. These meetings discussed the draft guidelines of the bishops on the mandate calling for all Catholics who teach Catholic theological disciplines in a Catholic college or university to have a mandate from the local bishop.

Meanwhile, the CTSA's own committee reported to the board. This report with many other documents was sent to all CTSA members and to all the U.S. bishops. At a meeting of the Pilarczyk committee with bishops and some representatives of the CTSA, ACCU, CLSA, and other groups, President Kenneth Himes summarized the approach of the CTSA. The conscience of the theologian who does not apply for the mandate or who refuses one that is offered should be respected. It is not a sign that such a theologian is not in communion with the Church. The mandate is a matter between the theologian and the bishop. Consequently, the bishop should not inform the college or university which theologians have or do not have the mandate. The mandate should not be incorporated into the bylaws of a school as a requirement for faculty. On another occasion, President Himes emphasized to the bishops that third-party "watchdog" groups, such as the now defunct website mandatum.org, should receive no support or cooperation from the bishops (2001, 217–18).

All of this occurred before the June 2001 meeting of the CTSA. The CTSA at the meeting decided to initiate conversations with the ACCU about the mandate. It also encouraged publications from its members explaining the nature, purpose, and function of Catholic theologians and the different settings in which theologians work—the university as distinct from the seminary, graduate school as distinct from undergraduate, theology as distinct from catechetics (2001, 216–18).

Meanwhile, on June 15, 2001, the bishops published their "Guidelines Concerning the Academic *Mandatum* (Canon 812)," calling for the need of a mandate for all who teach theological disciplines in a Catholic college or university. The guidelines developed in this document are to be renewed after five years. These guidelines also spell out the grounds for withholding or withdrawing the mandate, which include a presumption of right intention and conduct on the part of the teacher. An elaborate due process procedure is also spelled out.[3]

At the 2002 CTSA meeting, the president reported that the mandate requirement took effect on May 31, 2002. Meanwhile, the president had conversations with the ACCU. The executive director of the ACCU, Monika Helwig, asked to be kept abreast of any difficulties that CTSA members may have experienced so that she could inform the college and university presidents. President Peter Phan and others met with the chair of the bishops' doctrinal committee and decided that such meetings should occur annually in order to have a better working relationship.

Thus, the stage was set for what would happen in practice. The story of the CTSA has documented the basic tension in the relationship between theology and authority, between theologians and bishops. But these inevitable tensions exist within a common commitment to the good of the Church and mutual respect. Would the bishops now use the mandate to keep some theologians from teaching in Catholic colleges and universities?

So, what happened in practice? The CTSA has reported no problems about the grant or withdrawal of the mandate. No major controversies have been reported in the secular or religious press. From my observations and conversations with others, there have been no controversies. Some conservative Catholic institutions have publicly proclaimed they are accepting the mandate, and the theologians there seem to be in agreement. In some dioceses, the bishop just sent a mandate to all theologians working in Catholic higher education. Many theologians have not applied for the mandate, and no action has been taken against them. Thus, what could have been a very contentious situation never occurred. The long and acrimonious debate about the mandate has ended with a practical compromise that has avoided any controversy.

Why was there no disastrous controversy? One can only attempt to understand why the bishops did not use the mandate legislation to target some theologians. From the very beginning, the bishops were reluctant to get involved in the mandate controversy. *Ex corde* was released in 1990. The bishops took no action until 2001. The bishops' first document made no mention of the mandate, but the Vatican insisted they had to incorporate the mandate. This controversy did not just involve the bishops and the theologians. The presidents of Catholic colleges and universities were heavily involved. The leaders of the largest and best Catholic colleges and universities agreed with the Land O'Lakes Statement of 1967: "To perform its teaching and research functions effectively, the Catholic university must have a true autonomy and academic freedom in the face of authority of any kind, lay or clerical, external to the academic community itself."[4] These Catholic college presidents were committed to academic freedom and the autonomy of the college and university. Another important factor was that at this time the bishops were heavily involved in the controversy of their not removing pedophile priests from ministry. They certainly did not want another attention-getting controversy. However, there very well could have been a "loose cannon" bishop who felt compelled to take on the issue of denying or withdrawing a canonical mission in his diocese, but this has not occurred. The canonical mandate became a dead issue.

The fact that the canonical mandate for all practical purposes was not a problem in practice is verified in a 2015 article on *Ex corde Ecclesiae*. Jason King begins the article by recounting that he was on the job market in 2001, and at every interview he was asked about the mandate. There seemed to be general agreement that the mandate was and would continue to be the most important issue facing theologians in Catholic higher education. Such, however, was not the case. Articles have not been written about the mandate and subsequent controversies never developed.[5]

Three particular aspects of the tension between theologians and the magisterium, or Church authority, concern the actions of the Congregation for the Doctrine of the Faith against members of the CTSA, the actions of the Committee on Doctrine of the U.S. bishops, and the actions that occurred at a particular institution. The Congregation for the Doctrine of the Faith took action against Roger Haight, SJ, and Margaret A. Farley, RSM, during this twenty-five-year time frame. In December 2004, the

Congregation for the Doctrine of the Faith issued a notification that Roger Haight's 1999 book, *Jesus, Symbol of God*, contained serious doctrinal errors and concluded that until such time as the serious errors are corrected, Haight may not teach Catholic theology.[6] The CTSA board of directors issued a statement expressing their profound distress at the actions taken against Roger Haight. The statement goes on to make three points. First, Haight has done a great service in framing a crucial question and has engaged in constructive and critical dialogue about his position, including an open forum about his book at the 2002 CTSA convention. He has thus engaged in the internal debate and mutual correction of theologians called for by the magisterium. The statement criticizes the existing processes of the CDF as not affording the theologian an opportunity to clarify possible misunderstandings. The CDF should intervene as a last resort only after internal theological debate has failed. The action against Haight fails to recognize the important distinction between theology and catechetics ("Board of Directors Statement on Reverend Roger Haight, SJ," at Board Statements on the CTSA website).

Apparently, there were some conversations behind the scenes between the CDF and the Jesuit leadership in Rome. There were no further public actions taken by the CDF, but in the spring of 2008, Haight was ordered to stop teaching and publishing on theology but was allowed to write on spirituality. Haight has basically complied with the order but continues to do some teaching at Union Theological Seminary in New York City and has published a number of significant works since that time.[7] Throughout this long ordeal, Haight has not spoken publicly.

On June 4, 2012, the CDF declared that *Just Love* by Margaret Farley, RSM, *emerita* from Yale University, does not conform to the teachings of the magisterium and cannot be used as a valid expression of Catholic teaching, either in counseling or in formation or in ecumenical and religious dialogue. Farley was first informed that her book was under investigation two years earlier and has twice responded to the congregation's concerns.[8] At the June 2012 meeting, the president presented to the convention the statement of the board about the condemnation of *Just Love*. The fact that the book disagrees with some magisterial teaching is simply factual. Many faithful Catholics are raising questions similar to those of Professor Farley. The Notification gives the impression that there is no role for works of theology that give voice to the concern of many believers or that raise questions about the persuasiveness of certain teachings and that offer alternative theological frameworks. The convention passed a resolution proposed from the floor that the society endorse the statement of the board (2012, 171–72).

There have also been some interventions of the Committee on Doctrine of the U.S. bishops regarding the works of Catholic theologians who are members of the CTSA. At the 1996 meeting, a resolution originally submitted by members of the theology department of the University of Notre Dame deplored the fact that the bishops' committee failed to give "formal doctrinal dialogue" in accord with their Doctrinal Responsibilities document before publishing their observations regarding Richard McBrien's revised and updated *Catholicism* published in 1994. The meeting passed this and related resolutions with a clear but not unanimous vote (1996, 325).

There have been several more recent condemnations of the works by members of the CTSA by the Committee on Doctrine of the bishops. These have concerned the writings of Daniel Maguire, Peter Phan, Todd Salzmann, and Michael Lawler.[9] From what is known, it appears that in these cases the bishops did not follow their own procedures described in Doctrinal Responsibilities about various levels of dialogue with authors involved before there is any juridical action that is taken. The CTSA was, however, involved in the case involving Elizabeth Johnson. In this case, the president reported that she had received a number of emails from Johnson's colleagues at Fordham, past presidents of the CTSA, and others urging the CTSA to respond to this case. Professor Johnson herself did not ask anything from the CTSA. This explanation helps to explain why the CTSA did get involved in the earlier case of McBrien and now in the case of Johnson.

Elizabeth Johnson received a twenty-one-page document from the doctrinal committee of the bishops indicating that her book *Quest for the Living God* contained "misrepresentations, ambiguities, and errors that bear upon the faith of the Catholic Church." The board felt that the bishops' document reflected an extremely narrow understanding of theology to which they had to respond. Specifically, the bishops failed to follow the procedures they accepted in Doctrinal Responsibilities, they misrepresented her work by claiming that her book fails to take the faith of the Church as a starting point, and they made an incredible leap in logic by maintaining that her assertion that human words can never completely understand the divine reality means that God is unknowable. The business meeting passed a resolution that the bishops in this case once again did not follow their own procedures that had been worked out after much dialogue with the CTSA and the CLSA. Consequently, the resolution called on the bishops to set up a committee to evaluate the procedures of the Committee on Doctrine that led to this document (2011, 203–4, 207).

Elizabeth Johnson had been told that the bishops' committee was open to dialogue, so she wrote the committee a response to their document. On October 11, 2011, the committee responded to Johnson's observations and asserted that her book was not faithful to Catholic teaching. The CTSA board issued a statement expressing their dismay that the bishops' committee made no effort to engage Johnson personally and constructively in dialogue (2012, 169).

This discussion of the involvement of the CTSA in responding to the actions of the CDF and of the U.S. bishops concerning theologians raises questions that at least must be discussed without interfering with the story of the CTSA itself. Why did the bishops' committee not follow the procedures they overwhelmingly accepted for dealing with such disputes? The answer in some circumstances (regarding not just the cases discussed by the CTSA) could very well be that the bishops were told by the Vatican to take such actions. Many questions have been raised about the processes followed by the CDF, but there is also a question about why some and not other theologians were condemned. There is some evidence pointing to the fact that the CDF interferes when their action could be effective. Major Catholic universities in the United States, for example, would not act in accord with the CDF directives. This very well might explain why no theologians from such institutions have been condemned in any way by the CDF.

It seems there was only one instance of the CTSA criticizing an institution for terminating a faculty member, and this occurred early in this twenty-five-year period. Sister Barbara Fiand was removed from a faculty position at the Athanaeum of Ohio—the major seminary of the Archdiocese of Cincinnati. The proposed resolution calls for due process, which recognizes the rights of the faculty member to know the identity of the accuser and the content of the accusation. With a friendly amendment from the floor, the resolution passed unanimously (1998, 188).

There was one other action that does not fit into the categories already mentioned. In the 1994 apostolic letter *Ordinatio Sacerdotalis*, Pope John Paul II declared that the Church has no authority whatsoever to confer priestly ordination on women. This judgment is to be definitively held by all the Church's faithful. A response from the CDF in April 1995 maintained that this teaching has been taught infallibly by the ordinary and universal magisterium (1998, 197). The CTSA board established a task force that made an eight-page report, "Tradition and Ordination of Women," published in the 1998 *Proceedings* (1998, 197–204). The task force report summarized the apostolic letter and the later response of the CDF (see above). The report does not deal with the issue of the ordination of women but with the contention that the teaching is definitive or infallible. The report discusses Scripture, tradition, and the assertion that the teaching against the ordination of women is infallibly taught by the ordinary and universal magisterium. The report concludes that there are serious doubts about the nature of the authority of the teaching and calls for further study and discussion.

The resolution proposed by the board to the 1998 meeting called for acceptance of the conclusions of the report. The president announced there would be a paper ballot vote and that he as an interested party would step down from the chair. Such an unusual procedure shows how controversial this issue was thought to be. The resolution from the board was slightly modified at the meeting. The core of the resolution simply repeats the conclusion of the task force report that there are serious doubts that the teaching against the ordination of women has been infallibly taught and requires the definitive assent of the faithful. The final vote was: 216 yes, 22 no, and 10 abstentions (1998, 193–94).

This section has discussed the many tensions in the relationship of theologians with bishops in the twenty-five-year time frame from 1996 to 2020. But these tensions are only one part of the story. The CTSA explicitly worked to have a good relationship with the bishops. The local bishop was always invited to the opening session of the convention to give words of welcome. Practically every convention in this time frame reported on the annual meeting between the CTSA representatives and the Committee on Doctrine of the U.S. bishops. To cite each of these reports would be needlessly repetitious, but they show the constant concern of the CTSA to work together with the bishops. Such meetings also occurred at times with the Canadian bishops (2010, 193). At their October 2012 meeting, the board approved giving $500 each to ten groups of theologians for a dinner meeting with the local bishop. Most of the groups met and reported that the meetings went very well (2013, 178). At the 2016 convention, the president reported there were four proposals for the $500 grant for dinner meetings between theologians and the local bishop in the previous year. He urged the members to be more intentional about arranging such meetings (2016, 163).

On one occasion, however, both the attempt at collaboration and the tension appeared at approximately the same time. At its June 2012 meeting, the board agreed that in the interest of promoting better understanding, the president and president-elect would ask for a special meeting with Cardinal Donald Wuerl, the chair of the Committee on Doctrine. Wuerl readily agreed. The meeting on October 7 lasted seventy minutes and discussed all pertinent issues, including the recent document about Elizabeth Johnson. The meeting was described as mutually respectful and cordial. Four days after the meeting, the bishops' committee released their second response to Elizabeth Johnson saying her book was not faithful to Catholic teaching (2012, 168, 169). The response of the CTSA board to this action was described above.

The very reality of the relationship between theologians and the magisterium and between the CTSA and the bishops will always experience some tensions. But the CTSA has made a determined effort to respect the roles of the magisterium and the bishops and to collaborate with them. Yes, the roles by definition will involve some tensions, but they also exist within a broader commitment to the good of the Church.

THEOLOGICAL CONTENT

This chapter follows the outline of the previous chapters by first discussing the internal life of the CTSA and now the theological content of the presentations given at the conventions.

Two comments about the theological content of the conventions are in order. First, the *Proceedings*, originally published in print but then later available only online, published comparatively few of the papers actually given at any convention. Recall that the conventions during this time frame followed the same general structure. There were the presidential address and three plenary papers, but also about forty breakout sessions divided into invited sessions, sessions selected from proposals from the membership, topic sessions, and interest groups. The forty breakout sessions served several important purposes. They enabled members to come together for dialogue and discussion with those who shared the same field or interest group. The greater number of such sessions enabled many members to present papers at the conventions. In this connection, institutions were often willing to give financial support to those faculty who gave papers at professional academic meetings such as that of the CTSA. But the number of well over fifty papers (many breakout sessions had more than one paper) made it impossible to publish all of the papers given at the convention. The approach that was generally followed called for the *Proceedings* to publish the presidential address and the plenary papers together with possible responses to the plenaries, but to publish only a very short summary of less than two pages about what transpired in the breakout sessions. Thus, for all practical purposes, the pool of convention papers is quite small and gives only an extremely limited idea of the theological content discussed at each convention.

Second, all of these conventions had a theme proposed by the president-elect. The theme determined the content of the plenary papers and also many of the invited and selected sessions. The theme thus determined and limited the topics of the papers presented every year. As a result, the theology papers presented at the conventions in no way mirrored the work of Catholic theologians writing at this time.

Despite the small number of full papers found in the *Proceedings*, it is still impossible here to consider all the plenaries and presidential addresses in any depth. As mentioned earlier, I have decided it is better to go into some depth rather than just to mention very briefly the content of the papers that were delivered. As a result, I have chosen to consider the following four areas—the tensions between the magisterium and theologians and related but broader ecclesiological issues, theologies from the margins, ecology, and Church-world relationships.

Tensions concerning the Hierarchical Magisterium and Theologians

The tensions involving the hierarchical and papal magisterium and theologians continued to be present in this third twenty-five-year period of the life of the CTSA. But such tensions were somewhat less than in the previous time frame for several reasons, including the fact that there were fewer papal documents evoking such tensions. In the first few years of the time frame, the issues were quite similar to the issues that arose previously. The first topics considered in this section come from the special session of papers by Avery Dulles of Fordham and Richard A. McCormick of Notre Dame at the 1999 convention and the 2000 presidential address of Margaret Farley of Yale. As time went on, more general issues touching on the magisterium came to the fore. This section will consider the 2014 presidential address of Richard Gaillardetz on Pope Francis, two papers from the 1999 convention on the development of doctrine, and John Burkhard's 2015 paper on the *sensus fidelium*.

Avery Dulles and Richard McCormick gave papers at a special preconvention session on "The Nature and Authority of Doctrine: A Search for Common Ground" at the 1999 convention. This special session took place from one thirty to three thirty on Thursday afternoon before the preconvention Women's Seminar. Despite the early preconvention time, over two hundred attended the session. Why the great number of attendees? Dulles and McCormick were senior figures who had played major roles in U.S. Catholic theology—Dulles in ecclesiology and McCormick in moral theology. In the beginning, they often were in agreement, but later there arose some disagreements. In light of the importance of this session, the two opening papers were published in the *Proceedings*, which were at that time generally limited to the plenaries and the presidential addresses. Dulles's paper, "Catholic Doctrine between Revelation and Theology," addressed the proper response to three levels of magisterial teaching described in the 1998 *motu proprio* of Pope John Paul II, *Ad tuendam fidem*—doctrine infallibly taught as revealed, teaching infallibly taught as inseparably connected with revelation, and authentic noninfallible teaching. The differences today in the issue of the proper response to doctrinal teaching constitute a major fault line in contemporary Catholic theology, which runs the risk of producing a virtual schism within the Church itself. Today, there are even challenges to the first level of doctrines infallibly taught as revealed by some prominent theologians who identify divine revelation as an ecstatic encounter with God that has no doctrinal content. Some theologians today also object to the second level of infallible doctrines inseparably linked with revelation as an unwarranted extension of infallibility. Regarding the third level of authentic noninfallible teaching, the proper response is the *obsequium religiosum*. In particular, this means that dissent should be rare, reluctant, and respectful. Public dissent in the Church is not something desirable and normal. Dulles questions if anything can justify organized resistance, press conferences, soliciting signatures to petitions, and setting dissenters up as a kind of alternative magisterium (1999, 83–90).

McCormick's essay, "Moral Doctrine: Stability and Development," deals only with noninfallible teaching and dissent. Noninfallible teaching enjoys the presumption of truth, but it has a provisional character, entails the possibility of error, and dissent is justified for sufficient reasons. He emphasizes dissent because some type of dissent is necessary for development and also because there is a deliberate institutional attempt to nourish considerations hostile to dissent. McCormick agrees with an earlier statement by Dulles that Vatican II implicitly taught the legitimacy and value of dissent. (Dulles himself in these later writings pulled back from some of his earlier positions.) McCormick then briefly discusses the dissent from *Humanae vitae*'s teaching. He justifies such dissent and sees the possibility of development in seeing the inseparability of the unitive and procreative aspects of marital sexuality not in the individual act but as characteristic of the marital relationship as a whole (1999, 92–100).

McCormick's article was concise and very clear, bringing together many of the points he had made over the previous thirty years. It did not break more new ground. It seems to indicate there was no new ground to break. The debate about dissent from noninfallible teaching had been going on for three decades, and there was little or nothing new that could be said. This explains why these precise issues were not really discussed in the CTSA in the first two decades of the twenty-first century.

Margaret Farley in her presidential address in 2000, "The Church in the Public Forum: Scandal or Prophetic Witness?," dealt with the role of the Church in the contemporary public forum in the United States. There is general agreement among

Catholics on the goal for addressing public policy by the U.S. bishops—to build consensus so that society will care about the poor, marginalized, and vulnerable and to promote the freedom and well-being of all. There are, however, two issues that undermine the Church's work in the public forum—the preoccupation with abortion law and the scandal of repression of thought in the disciplining of theologians within the Church itself. With regard to abortion, Farley's point is not to remove abortion from the Church's agenda but to remove it as the primary priority in the bishops' agenda. The Church's positions on contraception, women, and feminism raise issues about the credibility of the Church in making abortion the primary public issue. One must also recognize the very important distinction between law and morality in the question of abortion. The abortion issue unfortunately overshadowed many of the other important public positions taken by the U.S. bishops. They are often forgotten and overlooked in light of the emphasis placed on abortion.

The second obstacle involves the Church's heavy emphasis on repressing thought and disciplining theologians, which weakens the voice of the Church in the public arena by awakening the old and even continuing fears among Americans about the Church's overall agenda. These two issues or obstacles undermine the public agenda of the Church in the United States, but there are resources in the Catholic tradition that can move from the scandal of the two issues to a truly prophetic witness of the Church in American public life today (2000, 87–101).

Ironically, as noted in the section on the internal life of the CTSA, Margaret Farley in March 2010 was informed she was under investigation by the CDF because of her book *Just Love: A Framework for Christian Sexual Ethics*. She corresponded with the CDF in the subsequent months. Finally, on June 4, 2012, the CDF concluded that her book is not a valid expression of Catholic teaching and cannot be used for teaching and counseling purposes.[10] Nothing, however, was said about her as a person, a theologian, a member of the Church, and a Sister of Mercy. While such an investigation lasts, the person involved is under a cloud and can never be sure what the final result will be. In her case, the result was less problematic than in others. In addition, there is the public scandal that she herself discussed in her 2000 presidential address.

In the twenty-first century, papers at the CTSA addressed three significant aspects of ecclesiology, which are important in themselves but also have ramifications for the narrower issue of the relationship between the hierarchical magisterium and theologians—the ecclesiology of Pope Francis, the development of doctrine, and the *sensus fidelium*.

In describing the internal life of the Church before 1996 to the present, the first part of this chapter pointed out the tensions between the magisterium and theologians in the pontificates of Popes John Paul II and Benedict XVI. These tensions were not, however, present in the early pontificate of Francis. In his 2014 presidential address, "The 'Francis Moment': A New Kairos for Catholic Ecclesiology," Richard Gaillardetz of Boston College shows how Pope Francis had insisted on five features of Vatican II that offer promise for realizing Vatican II's reform agenda. Gaillardetz points out that Francis in his early days had not proposed a developed ecclesiology but had emphasized five aspects of ecclesiology that did not receive that much emphasis in the previous thirty years of the papacy. One, in place of the centrality of *communio*, the primary metaphor for understanding the Church is the pilgrim people of God. Two, a missiological vision of the Church as centrifugal calls for Christians to enter into a deeper and more profound solidarity with the world. Three, a listening Church will involve an honest dialogue, as well as a certain messiness in the life of the Church itself. Four, ecclesial subsidiarity requires a greater role for the national conferences of bishops and the local Church. Five, the pastorality of doctrine insists that doctrine must be interpreted in relation to the core Christian kerygma in the light of concrete historical, cultural, and pastoral contexts. Gaillardetz recognizes that only time will tell how this papal vision of the Church can be transformed into an effective program for Church reform (2014, 63–80).

The theme of the 1999 convention was "The Development of Doctrine"—a most significant issue. This discussion will consider just two of the plenary papers—those of John E. Thiel and John T. Noonan Jr. Thiel of Fairfield University treats the topic of the development of doctrine from the standpoint of systematic theology's understanding of tradition. Thiel describes his position as a retrospective conception of tradition as opposed to a prospective conception. The prospective approach starts with the apostolic tradition and sees the future in the light of the apostolic tradition. The prospective approach understands continuity to be preserved by a chronological handing over of the apostolic tradition down through the centuries. A more romantic approach to the prospective view began in the nineteenth century and is accepted by many theologians today, such as Karl Rahner and Edward Schillebeeckx. This approach sees continuity not by literally handing over the apostolic tradition but by the latent awakening of the apostolic tradition that manifests itself gradually in historical forms. A strong argument against such prospective approaches is the doctrine of the immaculate conception of Mary. History shows that the immaculate conception was not held in continuity with the apostolic tradition. For example, Thomas Aquinas himself did not accept the immaculate conception.

Thiel proposes a retrospective concept of tradition that begins with the present moment looking back to the past. In this understanding, continuity comes when a particular retrospection is claimed as tradition by the whole Church. One begins with a particular that then, through the Spirit, is accepted by the whole

Church. From beginning with the particular today, one moves to communal acceptance by the whole Church. Because of this, the retrospective approach is not relativistic. Time will tell how subsequent theologians deal with Thiel's newer retrospective approach to tradition.

John T. Noonan Jr., in his paper "Experience and the Development of Moral Doctrine," insists on the place of experience in the development involving change of particular moral doctrines. Noonan discusses the following illustrations of how change has occurred—the indissolubility of marriage, usury, death penalty, state persecution of heretics, and slavery. Noonan himself has written extensively and in-depth on many of these issues. In all of these cases, what are the experiences that counted? There is first the experience of the people who were subject to these laws or positions, and then the experience of the decision makers. At least since the twelfth century, the decision makers have been an identifiable body of theologians and canonists subject to the supervision of popes and bishops. Raw experience is not enough.

The theme of the 2015 convention was "The *Sensus Fidelium.*" The most significant paper from our perspective is John Burkhard's "The *Sensus Fidelium*: Old Questions, New Challenges" (2015, 27–43). Burkhard develops his paper in three stages. First, Vatican II insisted on a listening Church, and this replaced the understanding of the two parts of the Church as the teaching Church and the learning Church. Dialogue should characterize the life of the total Church. Second, according to Vatican II, the *sensus fidelium* and ecclesiology involve a number of important aspects. The primary metaphor of the total Church is the people of God. The pilgrim people of God is the horizon from which all other understandings of the Church are viewed. Vatican II also insisted that the threefold office of priest, teacher, and ruler is the primary way of understanding the role of office and ministry in the Church. All members of the Church share in these threefold functions. Such an understanding replaces the older twofold "powers of order and jurisdiction" belonging only to the hierarchy. All the people of God share in the prophetic and especially the teaching role of Jesus. Vatican II understands the church as *communio* (*koinonia*). *Communio* calls for conversation not only from the top down but also from the bottom up. An excellent illustration of this *communio* was the structured dialogical process the U.S. bishops used in writing their pastoral letters on peace and the economy in the 1980s. The *communio ecclesiarum* must include the local church, the regional church, and the Church universal. The faithful need to have a real sense of ownership with regard to all these levels of the churches. Third, in the Vatican II document *Dei Verbum*, the *sensus fidelium* (although the exact word is not used) is more than a static *locus theologicus*. The faithful perform an indispensable role in more deeply preserving the truth and more effectively applying it to life. As practical and experience based, the *sensus fidelium* is also participatory knowledge. Some truths can only be known by the knower being immersed in them and living from them. In conclusion, the *sensus fidelium* has an important role in knowing God's truth and striving to live it out in daily life.

Minorities

As in the previous twenty-five-year period, there was also an emphasis now on minorities and racial and ethnic groups on the margins. One new reality that came to the fore after 1996 was the recognition of white privilege and white racism.

In a 2001 plenary, Margaret Guider of Boston College discusses racism and white supremacy in light of the general theme of *Missio ad Gentes*. One of the major obstacles impeding the missionary vocation of the Church throughout the world is the counterwitness of Christians. The multifaceted reality of racism is an insidious problem throughout our world and the complicity of Christians in the perpetuation of racist attitudes, endeavors, and social structures is a primary impediment to evangelization.

Racism is a problem in the world. Guider understands racism as a system by which one race maintains supremacy over another through a set of attitudes, behaviors, social structures, ideologies, and the requisite power to impose these ideas. In the context of North America and Europe, racism has largely been understood as a system of white supremacy and white superiority. The multifaceted and insidious problem of racism continues to take a toll on human life and human relationships throughout the world.

Racism is a powerful counterwitness in the Church. Yes, the white Church has issued documents condemning racism as a sin. With some exceptions, however, ecclesial statements on racism tend to reveal a Church that is self-referentially white and speaks in a white voice. There must be some way for the whole Church of history to collectively acknowledge the counterwitness to the gospel before the world, confess its sin of racism to the Church of faith, and ask for forgiveness and do penance. In a closing section, Guider appeals to the moral imagination to overcome the scandal of racist counterwitness in so many followers of Jesus and of the Church itself.

The 2003 convention enthusiastically responded to the presidential address of Jon Nilson, "Confessions of a White Catholic Racist." The racism of white Catholic theologians consists of ignoring, marginalizing, and dismissing the body of theological thought and challenge based on the Black struggle for justice. Nilson of Loyola of Chicago admits he is a racist because he has rarely read and never cited any Black theology in his many writings. Occasionally, he has assigned a short article on Black theology to his students, but never an entire book. He has learned much from feminist and Latin American liberation theologians but paid little attention to Black theology. Nilson concludes this section by remarking there are many white Catholic racist theologians. As mentioned in chapter 3, in the early 1970s the CTSA recognized the importance of Black theology. Preston Williams of Harvard in his 1973 plenary address urged the society to find, mentor, and promote Black Catholic theologians. President Richard McBrien in 1974 appointed a research committee for Black theology under chair Joseph Nearon, who was the only Black member of the CTSA at that time. This approach awakened Nearon to recognize Catholic theology in the United States as racist.

Two reasons help to explain Catholic theological racism. First, the realities of segregation, and residential segregation also present in the North after the influx of Black people from the South, constituted the main obstacle to Black social advancement. As a result of segregation and white flight, few Catholics and few Catholic theologians had a friendly relationship with a Black person. Throughout the formative years of contemporary Catholic theologians, we saw no faces of the intolerable suffering of Black persons. Second, integration was proposed as the ideal. Integration was the cry of the Civil Rights Movements of the 1950s and later. The particular Catholic emphasis on integration was assimilation. Just as Irish, Italians, and Poles were assimilated into American society, so would Black people be. Such an approach failed to acknowledge the destructive features of Black history in the United States, which made assimilation very difficult. Progressive Catholics, such as John LaFarge, SJ, insisted on the primacy of assimilation and in the process took over what had been the work of the Federated Colored Catholics under Thomas Wyatt Turner, who insisted that Catholic Blacks should be the agents of their own advancement. Assimilation took away the Black voice in the Catholic Church.

Two other factors offer some explanation why Catholics paid no attention to Black theology, but they in no way justify the failure of white Catholic theologians to engage Black theology. The Black struggle for justice in the United States coincided with the time of Vatican II and its all-embracing influence on U.S. Catholic theologians. Catholic theologians were absorbed with trying to assimilate the work of Vatican II into their theology. There were also features of Black theology that can explain but never justify the failures of white Catholic theology. Black theology from its beginnings was closely associated with Black Power and Black Separatism. Black theology was for Black people and exhibited anger and hostility to privileged whites. Black theology also appealed to nontraditional sources, such as Black spirituals. In addition, Catholic theologians were interested in a systematic and ordered theology, whereas Black theology did not want a system, but a radical change.

Nilson maintains that a substantial and critical engagement with Black theology is indispensable for a truly *catholic* theology. Such a truly catholic theology must be in dialogue with Black theology. But the first step for white Catholic theologians is to recognize our sin of racism with all its dimensions and the failure of the Church to recognize these sins in the past and the blatant failures in our history.

Selected sessions in 2002 and 2003 dealt with white privilege, but as was the custom, only brief summaries of the papers were given. In 2004, Laurie Cassidy and Alex Mikulich started a developing group to reflect on the issues of white privilege and racism. In 2007, Cassidy and Mikulich edited a volume of papers given at these sessions.[11] Bryan Massingale's 2010 presidential address, "*Vox Victimarum, Vox Dei*: Malcolm X as a Neglected Classic for Catholic Theological Reflection," calls for Catholic theologians to take Malcolm X as a dialogue partner. Massingale, now of Fordham, confesses that his own reading of Malcolm thoroughly shook him. Massingale in his book *Racial Justice and the Catholic Church* dialogued especially with James Cone.

But now he sees the need to listen to the more radical Malcolm X. Malcolm at first sight seems to be a very unlikely dialogue partner. Malcolm is devastating in his critique of America and the Christian Church. He proudly describes himself not as an American but as a victim of Americanism. Christianity is a white Church with a white God that brings about a dual brainwashing—rendering whites unaware of the horrors of racial oppression and Black people passive in their roles. But Massingale sees Malcolm in light of the adage that the voice of victims is the voice of God—*vox victimarum, vox Dei*. Malcolm's work fits David Tracy's understanding of a classic because it has the power to transform the horizon of the interpreter and disclose new meanings and experiential possibilities.

Malcolm sees Black people in the United States as full of self-hatred and inner wounding because of their oppressive situation—a plight he describes as psychological castration. Blacks have to develop a critical consciousness that makes them aware of the truth of their situation. Catholic social ethicists and Pope John Paul II have called for the importance of solidarity, but their understanding of solidarity underestimates both the recalcitrance of the privileged and the political passivity of the dispossessed. In a life-changing visit to the holy sites of Islam, Malcolm claimed that maybe white Americans might accept the oneness of all human beings. The later Malcolm revised his earlier position and saw a role for white Americans in religion and the struggle. Whites can and should be on the battle lines where America's racism really is, and that is in their own white communities. Authentic solidarity cannot evade social conflict, resistance, and recalcitrance if it is to be of genuine service in the quest for social transformation (2010, 63–68).

Black theology's appearance at the CTSA started slowly, but in this time frame between 1996 and 2020, it grew in breadth and depth. At this time, racism and white privilege also came to the fore. Also in this time frame, very often there were breakout sessions of one type or another dealing with Black theology.

Latinx approaches (a word that embraces both Latina and Latino) had developed in the previous time frame, obviously occasioned by the fact that there were so many Latinx people in the United States and a growing number of Latinx Catholic theologians. At the 2008 convention with the theme of "Generations," M. T. (Maria Theresa) Dávila speaking as a second-generation Latinx theologian gave a paper entitled "Catholic Hispanic Theology in the United States: *Dimensiones de la Opción Preferencial por los Pobres en el Norte.*" The first section summarizes her understanding of Catholic Hispanic theology in the first generation, which roughly corresponds to what was treated in chapter 3 of this book. The first generation was responding to the overwhelming transformation in the American Catholic Church where one out of every two Catholics is of Hispanic descent. This theology involved a preferential option for culture attentive to the "everyday-ness of life" on the margins in the United States. The emphasis was on *lo cotidiano*, attention to daily experience; *fiesta*, the celebration of life as gift and resistance to oppression and death; *Nosotros Diginidad*, alternative visions of anthropology focusing on being rather than having; *mestizaje*, involving the history of violence and conquest; *religión popular*, the particular religious practices that sustain Hispanic people's lives.

The next generation believes that the first generation emphasized the cultural over the political and economic. Here Dávila appeals to Latin American liberation theology. There is need for a more radical approach that takes concepts like *lo cotidiano* as involving a critique of the systematic experience that keeps most of the world's population in oppressive and inhumane conditions. The U.S. theological academy desperately needs such a critique of the political economy. Latinx theology needs to be liberated and grounded on the preferential option for the poor. The final section of the paper suggests three areas that should be of concern to the Catholic theological community and for which Latinx theology offers a challenge and critical methodology. These three areas are engagement with civil society, especially in issues of race and immigration; issues of class and economy; and, finally, militarism, empire, and the culture of violence (2008, 28–48).

In his 2005 presidential address, "The Crucified and Risen Christ: From Calvary to Galilee," Roberto Goizueta of Boston College took the same basic approach as Dávila but from a different methodological perspective. The foundation for Christian belief is the gratuitous and incredible gift of God's love to us. Too many, even believers, reject this unimaginable gift and put their trust in burgeoning stockpiles of weapons, xenophobic immigration laws, compulsive consumerism, and addictions of all kinds. The lived faith of the poor helps us to understand the reality of God's love. The poor have discovered the liberating truth—that we are indeed loved, and that life is a gift and is therefore worth living no matter what. The crucified and risen Jesus is the sign of God's extravagant love for each of us.

What are the implications of this love embedded in the crucified and risen Jesus? Unless one has placed oneself on the side of the oppressed and feels with them, one cannot understand the gratuitous gift of God's love. In Caravaggio's painting, Jesus puts Thomas's hand into his own wound. Thomas thus makes explicit the necessity of acknowledging the suffering of the innocent victim and acknowledging complicity in that suffering. Too often today, people recoil from such suffering and do not want to put their hand into the wounds of Jesus. Many do not want to acknowledge their powerlessness, fragility, and mortality. This is what we learn from the encounter of Jesus with the disciples after the resurrection.

The disciples are called to Galilee where the community of faith will be revealed. Galilee has theological significance.

The Jewish establishment in Jerusalem looked down on Galilee because they considered these people ignorant about the law, contaminated by daily contact with pagans, and speaking not true Greek but a corrupt language. But it is precisely in the middle of contaminated, corrupt believers that the resurrected Christ will be encountered. Christ's resurrected body is present among the "impure," "corrupted" believers of Galilee, the lonely and rejected of this world (2005, 57–71).

Ecology

Ecology and the environment became important issues for theology in general and the CTSA in particular during this time frame. In 1996 in her presidential address, "Turn to the Heavens and the Earth: Retrieval of Cosmic Theology," Elizabeth Johnson of Fordham challenged the CTSA and Catholic theology in general to set off on a great intellectual adventure, one where both wisdom and prophecy will intertwine the way to a new theological synthesis and praxis. Ecology and cosmology are not just new, particular issues, but cosmology should be a framework within which all theological topics are rethought (1996, 13).

Johnson begins her essay by pointing out the longstanding Catholic heritage that reached its zenith in the twelfth and thirteenth centuries. Cosmology, anthropology, and the theology of God formed a harmonious unity, as illustrated in the works of Hildegard of Bingen, Bonaventure, and Thomas Aquinas. But after the fifteenth century, neither Catholic nor Protestant theology kept pace with new scientific worldviews. Instead, they focused on God and the self, leaving the world aside.

Johnson insists that the intellectual integrity of theology calls for recognizing all of creation. Ignoring the cosmos has had a deleterious effect, because it paves the way for theology to retreat to otherworldliness, to disparage matter (the body and the earth), and to offer interpretations of reality far removed from the way things actually work. Contemporary science is discovering a natural world that is surprisingly dynamic, organic, self-organizing, indeterminate, chancy, boundless, and open to the mystery of reality. Bringing in the new cosmology shifts the axis of all theological questions, setting an agenda for years to come. The new cosmology prods us to rethink basic questions but also offers a new framework in which to consider typical theological questions.

In addition to the intellectual reason for theology's turn to the heavens and earth, there is also a compelling moral reason. The human race is inflicting devastation on the life sphere of our world. This ongoing devastation of God's good earth perceived through the lens of theology bears the mark of deep sinfulness. Greed, self-interest, injustice, and the failure to think and act in the long term have brought about ecocide, geocide, and biocide—the new terms for the devastation of our planet Earth. We are all called to real conversion. The earth is not just an instrument for humans to use for their own narrow interest. Nature has its own inherent value coming from God. Exploitation of the earth is intimately connected with the exploitation of the poor and women in our world. Ecological devastation is an especially important moral issue that theology needs to address (1996, 1–14).

The theme of the 2017 convention was "Ecology: Theological Investigations." In keeping with the convention structure at this time, the plenary sessions and many of the invited and selected sessions dealt with this theme. We will consider the three plenary addresses given by Christiana Zenner Peppard, Denis Edwards, and Anne Clifford. Christiana Zenner Peppard of Fordham develops her paper, "An Ethics of Aridity: Theology, Ecology, and Planetary Change," in three stages—an overview of theological evaluations of ecology; an in-depth discussion of the ecological and water situation in Albuquerque where the CTSA meeting took place; and some multidimensional intersections of ecology, theology, and ethics with regard to water.

The first section describes the work of some Catholic theologians regarding ecology. She then mentions some involvements by Catholic groups with regard to water. Zenner Peppard calls her approach to this question of water the Anthropocene Paradox, which recognizes both the planetary aspect and the particular aspect of the water issue in specific and different contexts. This reflects the need to recognize both the planetary or universal aspects, as well as the specific and the particular.

The second section discusses the aridity of Albuquerque. New Mexico receives about eleven to thirteen inches of annual rainfall. An arid environment is less than ten inches and semi-arid is from ten to twenty inches of rainfall annually. The Albuquerque water situation is discussed in the light of five important factors related to water scarcity—pollution, groundwater loss, climate change, consumptive versus nonconsumptive use of water, and infrastructural dimensions.

The third and final section deals with the ethics of water. Zenner Peppard insists on some universality in an ethics of water because fresh water is sui generis and a sine qua non for life on this earth, including but not limited to the human. She is also an intersectional feminist who constantly asks what voices, values, and insights have been elided or ignored? People often speak about human rights to water, but critics argue that rights language is almost always based on Western philosophical assumptions that can be highly individualistic and anthropocentric in ways that imperil nonhuman entitlements. Zenner Peppard thinks about extending rights to animals and ecosystems. Pope Francis has even insisted on a right of the environment. In 2017, rivers in India and New Zealand have been granted legal rights status. All need to remember that human beings and many other forms of life are dependent on water (2017, 1–13).

Whereas Zenner Peppard emphasizes the scientific and the ethical, Denis Edwards in his paper, "Ecological Theology: Trinitarian Perspectives," emphasizes the theological and in particular the relation between the Trinity and the natural world. He begins with a description of the Great Barrier Reef (Edwards was an Australian), showing its abundance and diversity as well as its vulnerability. It is the largest living structure of our planet, which is believed to have begun its life twenty million years ago. The Reef supports a wonderful diversity of species and habitats from algae to marine turtles and whales. The Reef, however, is under extreme threat from four major causes—climate warming and its ramifications, poor water quality because of the runoff from agriculture and industry, coastal development, and illegal fishing. The Reef is a marvel of biological interrelationships, complexity, and diversity, which is a product of life on our planet. The paper then takes up insights on the relationship between the Trinity and the natural world from three points in trinitarian theology—its origins in Athanasius, its systematic presentation in Aquinas, and its contemporary evolutionary articulation.

For Athanasius, the Word and the Spirit all actively engage in the economy of creation and salvation. The green turtle swimming over the brilliantly colored Reef exists only because it partakes of the Wisdom/Word in the Spirit. The turtle is the self-expression of divine creation and bears the imprint of Holy Wisdom. The saving Word is the very same eternal Word in whom all things are created. The incarnation, death, and resurrection of Jesus bring about a deification of creation. The paper emphasizes the inclusion of the wider creation in deification. He does not make a total or sharp separation between the deification of human beings and the rest of creation. At times, he explicitly includes the whole of creation in the liberation that comes from Christ's resurrection.

Edwards focuses on three aspects of Aquinas's approach to the Trinity—the inner link between the trinitarian processions and the process of creation, the diversity of creation as the self-expression of the Trinity, and the relationship of creation in the light of the relations of the Trinity. The divine persons are subsistent relations. Take away the relations and nothing remains. Such an understanding sees the human being in relationships with God, with other humans, and with all of God's creatures.

His third perspective is an ecological and evolutionary theology of the Word and the Spirit in the twenty-first century that recognizes what we now know about the evolution of our world. The Spirit is the energy of love and evolutionary emergence. God's self-transforming love has the effect of setting creatures free to become. The Spirit is the energy of love enabling evolutionary emergence. The Word of God is the divine attractor in evolutionary emergence. There is no preordained divine plan. Edwards's trinitarian theology now sees the Wisdom/Word in which all things are created (Athanasius and Aquinas) and the Logos in whom are the forms of creation in an evolutionary perspective as the attractor of evolutionary emergence of the whole universe. Ecological conversion means seeing ourselves as part of a family and communion of creatures before God. This involves not only a radical transformation in how we see the wider natural world but also how we feel for it and with it. It involves a change in lifestyle, a new asceticism, new priorities, and personal and communal action. Edwards sees Pope Francis as endorsing such an understanding (2017, 14–28).

In a perceptive response to Edwards, Andrew Prevot fully supports trinitarian theology as a path to ecological conversion. To Edwards's use of trinitarian ontology in which each entity is recognized as a trace of the Trinity, we also need a trinitarian aesthetics that clarifies how different sorts of creatures are calling and crying to us and a trinitary ethic that connects the liberating word of Jesus with environmental justice movements (2017, 29–31).

The title of Anne Clifford's plenary address at the 2017 CTSA convention, "Pope Francis's *Laudato si'*," accurately describes what she does in her paper. Clifford, of Iowa State, is most appreciative of the pope's insistence on protecting planetary health and his bringing together the preferential option for the earth and the preferential option for the poor. Pope Francis notes two obstacles to integral ecology—an economic system focusing on short-term profit and a technological approach that sees nature as something to be exploited. Clifford, depending on some others, adds three more obstacles—the consequences of ecological devastation are not seen by many people; many pay no attention to the findings of environmental scientists, especially with regard to climate change; and the failure to recognize the role that gender patterns play in issues connected with environmental concerns. The majority of the world's hungry are not men but women and children. Women are disproportionately affected by weather and natural disasters.

From an ecofeminist perspective, it seems that the apex of creation in the encyclical is clearly man. The encyclical unfortunately uses exclusive language. Clifford also has some problems with the pope's insistence on Mother Earth. There is still a tendency for some to see women as identified with matter and the male with spirit or intellect. Most of the pope's sources are male, and his concerns are often those of males. There is no mention of ecofeminism in the encyclical. With this as a clue, Clifford then develops the ecofeminist approach of two authors—Ivone Gebara of Brazil and Wangari Muta Maathai of Kenya.

The presidential address of Elizabeth Johnson in 1996 and the plenary sessions at the 2017 convention are the bookends of the discussion of ecology at the CTSA in this period. There were many other breakout sessions dealing with ecology between these two bookends.

Church and World

Some of the papers already discussed deal with the relationship of the Church and the world. This section will discuss three papers—the 2004 presidential address of M. Shawn Copeland, the 2017 presidential address of David Hollenbach, and the 2019 plenary paper of Emily Reimer-Barry.

M. Shawn Copeland's 2004 presidential address, "Political Theology as Interruptive," takes a quite radical approach to the proper role of the Church and theology in the contemporary world. Copeland, of Boston College, bases her paper on an analysis of the world in which we live. Violence and brutality are ever-present; the social expression of our cultural meanings and values soaks in coarseness and vulgarity; our public institutions collapse under the selfish economic self-interests of elites who clearly thwart the survival, hope, and very lives of others. Religion itself and Catholic life and theology are often complicit in these attitudes. In this context, the role of theology is to be interruptive. Her paper brings together several difficult and dense topics, and it is impossible to deal well or in-depth with all the nuances that the gravity of the situation calls for. But in the light of the gospel, she feels the need to speak out. I describe her paper as a theological *cri de coeur*. Theology must become not only public but also political as it strives to interrupt what is occurring.

Her first step is to understand political theology as interruptive. Such was the approach in Germany from people like Jürgen Moltmann, Dorothy Sölle, and Johan Baptist Metz. Political theology based on following the crucified Jesus develops a Christian praxis of solidarity with all the victims of injustice, evokes a conversion of heart and living, and calls for an interruption of the violence, injustice, and self-interest so prevalent in our world. Unfortunately, with few exceptions, U.S. theologians have not developed such a political theology.

Copeland's understanding of political theology calls for a threefold interruption. The first is the interruption of spiritual and critical deformation, which is succinctly described as an emphasis on having rather than being. The second is an interruption within theology itself. The state of our national and global conditions moves to the fore our collaboration in opposing the injustice, greed, and self-interest that are so prevalent. Third, political theology is interruptive of violence. Violence is the coercive attempt to limit or thwart the exercise and realization of the essential and effective freedom of human persons and groups.

We as Christians must live out forgiveness and reconciliation. Political theology in our present situation in the United States calls for three new duties to interrupt the violence, injustice, and oppression so prevalent in our society—witness, memory, and lament. Witness in Greek is *martyr*. The witness of the martyr involves self-sacrifice and even death. We theologians must be willing to sacrifice—our comforts, our security, our joys, perhaps even our lives. Memory means for us to tell the story of those who have suffered, thus puncturing the historical amnesia that has forgotten so many and lance the infected memories that support the present attitudes. Lament is both a form of prayer and a practice of justice that announces loudly and publicly what is unjust in the here and now. We as theologians can no longer sit silently on the sidelines, but we must act in a hope rooted in the dangerous memory of the crucified Jesus of Nazareth.

David Hollenbach, of Georgetown, in his 2017 presidential address, "The Glory of God and the Global Common Good: Solidarity in a Turbulent World," takes a different approach from

Copeland. He develops the approach of Catholic social ethics by emphasizing the important role of the common good in bringing about justice on the local, regional, and global levels today. Hollenbach has written more on the common good than any other U.S. Catholic moral theologian.

Hollenbach begins by recognizing the turbulence in the world today. He describes the turbulence as local communities fractured by globalization and new technologies in the Global North; poverty, war, and displacement in the Global South; and environmental degradation everywhere. Antiglobalization sentiment has nationalistic and anti-Islamic dimensions. Notice that his description of the turbulence is not as deep or negative as the vision of Copeland.

The common good, local, regional, and global, provides the proper response to the present turbulence. The common good has a rich history in the Catholic social tradition, but often its meaning is quite vague. His understanding of the common good draws on the similarity to what economists call public goods. A public good is a good present to all members of the community when it is present for any of them. Such goods must be present for everyone, not just for the elite or the wealthy. For example, the public goods of peace or clean air or water are good for all the inhabitants of the community. The common good presupposes a relational anthropology and the importance of solidarity. Local, regional, and global solidarity are all necessary. Exclusionary localism, isolationist nationalism, and hegemonic globalism must be resisted. We need a network of crisscrossing communities to overcome the divisions and conflicts that exist and that leave far too many with no social support at all.

A final section links the striving for the common good in the social ministry of the Church and of Christians with the glory of God. This link between the common good and the glory of God was made by Ignatius of Loyola and is illustrated in the various ministries of the Jesuit order. The promotion of the common good is a way to show forth God's glory in the midst of history. The link between the common good and God's glory and righteousness begins to be present in making justice more present in human history, but the full visibility will only come at the end of time (2017, 51–60).

Emily Reimer-Barry's plenary address at the 2019 convention, "Another Pro-Life Movement Is Possible," can be accurately described as a rallying cry for a new pro-life movement. Reimer-Barry, of the University of San Diego, describes herself as pro-life, pro-women, and pro-justice. She does not challenge the magisterial teaching that there is a presumption against the taking of human life.

Reimer-Barry maintains that the pro-life movement her generation of Catholics inherited is deeply flawed and needs to be replaced. There have been some attempts at improving the bishops' approach to pro-life, but many huge problems remain. The campaign to overturn *Roe v. Wade* is rooted not in care and concern for women but in patriarchy that wants to control, dominate, and disempower women. The Church unfortunately does not believe that women's bodies matter, that women are capable of making good decisions, that the woman is best positioned to understand the circumstances of her life and what it is possible for her to do. In addition to patriarchy, the dominant Catholic right-to-life movement is guilty of a double standard of morality, oversimplification, and single-issue politics. The aim of her renewed right-to-life movement is not to overturn *Roe v. Wade* but rather to reduce the number of abortions. The existing pro-life movement seeks to undermine the moral agency of women and the intrinsic value of women. The renewed right-to-life movement most strongly supports the moral agency of women. Prioritizing the moral agency of women is an important value in itself, but it also serves as the way in which to try to reduce the number of abortions. The way to reduce abortions is not by law but by persuading women in their moral agency to respect life.

Unlike her inherited right-to-life movement, she recognizes that reducing the number of abortions calls for many other important changes in our society, such as affordable childcare, health care, a living wage, and pay for working women during their pregnancy. Catholic parishes and Catholic institutions should provide free or sliding-scale infant daycare. If we were to listen to why some women abort, we would recognize the problems created by poverty and work together for more equal distribution of wealth in our country and world. Reimer-Barry also sees the Catholic right-to-life movement working together with others, even Planned Parenthood, in trying to bring about conditions for a woman to recognize her moral agency. It should also be mentioned that she recognizes but does not stress that overturning *Roe v. Wade* will probably never happen (2019, 21–41).

In addition, the right-to-life movement must also be involved in all those other life issues that call for justice and equality in our society. A renewed right-to-life movement seeks to foster a culture and society that empowers pregnant women to be persuaded to choose life. Such a movement will not be easy, but that is the direction we should take.

The second part of this chapter follows the outline of the previous chapters discussing the content of the papers given at the annual conventions of the CTSA from 1995 to 2019. The four significant areas of theology covered here are the tensions between theologians and the hierarchical magisterium and related but broader ecclesiological issues, theology from the margins, ecology, and Church-world relationship.

CONCLUSION

The old adage wisely says that a picture is worth a thousand words. The fiftieth anniversary convention site of the CTSA had a picture of the first convention in 1946. The picture showed about one hundred members present, all of whom were priests in Roman collars. The fiftieth anniversary convention attracted more than five hundred members, and Roman collars were few and far between.

This book has shown the remarkable changes and developments in the first seventy-five-year history of the CTSA. This conclusion will try to explain this factual situation, showing why these changes occurred. Catholic theology serves three publics— the Church, the academy, and the broader human society and world. Developments in these three publics and theology's relationship to them help to understand how and why both the internal life of the CTSA and the theology discussed in the papers at the conventions have changed.

The primary public for Catholic theology is obviously the Catholic Church. Catholic theology is done in and for the Church. Events in the life of the Church have a great influence on theology. The most significant event in the first seventy-five years of the CTSA was the Second Vatican Council (1962–65). Vatican II ushered in a new era in Catholic theology. Preparatory documents for the council were proposed mostly by the existing congregations in the Roman curia, except for the document on the liturgy; all of these were rejected, and newer ones were proposed and developed by the council fathers. This is not the place to discuss Vatican II in detail, but this fact of the rejection of the proposed documents illustrates the substantial changes brought about by Vatican II in Catholic theology.

One significant change brought about by Vatican II was the importance of ecumenical dialogue. Recall that in the middle of the 1960s the CTSA conventions had discussions of particular issues by a Protestant and Catholic theologian. But later, Catholic theologians at the CTSA incorporated an ecumenical dimension into their approach to theology.

Vatican II greatly affected not only the theological content of the papers given at the CTSA conventions but also the internal life of the society. Beginning in 1970, the presidents of the society were younger theologians greatly influenced by Vatican II. Many of the older theologians dropped out of the theological enterprise here in the United States because they were not all that comfortable with the changes brought about by Vatican II.

The second most important ecclesial event affecting Catholic theology and the CTSA was *Humanae vitae*, the 1968 encyclical of Pope Paul VI reaffirming the condemnation of artificial contraception for spouses. The issue of dissent from noninfallible hierarchical teaching and the broader issue of the relationship between the hierarchical magisterium and theologians cast a long shadow over Catholic theology and the life of the CTSA. As developed in the previous chapters, these tensions were the primary issue in the internal life of the society since 1968. Actions taken by the Congregation for the Doctrine of the Faith against theologians were discussed and acted on by the members and officers of the CTSA. The papers given at the annual conventions often address these tensions and the broader issues of ecclesiology somewhat related to the role of theologians and the hierarchical magisterium in the life of the Church. The call for a mandate from the proper Church authority for those teaching theological disciplines in Catholic colleges and universities was the most discussed issue at the conventions of the CTSA in the 1990s and into the first year of the twenty-first century.

In addition to Vatican II and *Humanae vitae*, Catholic theologians paid attention to the teachings and actions of the hierarchical magisterium and frequently cited and commented on such teachings and actions. The papers given at the CTSA very often followed this approach. The primary public for Catholic theology is the Church, and the life and theological work of the CTSA in the first seventy-five year reflect this reality.

The second public of Catholic theology is the academy; the academy influenced the life of theology and of the CTSA in many ways. Before Vatican II, the home of Catholic theology in the United States was the seminary and the approach to theology was more pastoral than academic. After Vatican II, there has been a growing number of graduate programs in theology at many Catholic universities, whereas before Vatican II, for all practical purposes, the Catholic University of America had the only graduate program in this country. In basically the same time frame, there was a strong move sparked by what is now the College Theology Society to make the required courses in theology in Catholic undergraduate programs more academic. Before then, these courses were catechetical in nature and taught by ordained or vowed priests and religious who often had no advanced degrees in theology. In this context, Catholic theology became much more academic.

As a result, Catholic theologians today are much better trained than I was. They have a deeper and broader understanding of the discipline. Also, in an academic atmosphere, they are more at home with interdisciplinary approaches and bringing in this type of dialogue in their theological work. The academic ethos of theology has also contributed to the growth of the discipline. Professors in Catholic colleges are part of a system that not only encourages publication but also requires it for advancement. Tenure and promotion in Catholic universities and in the best of Catholic colleges require scholarly publications. The seminary ethos that characterized Catholic theology earlier did not promote or even require academic publication. As a result, today the discipline of Catholic theology has a depth and a breadth that it never had before.

The earlier chapters of this book showed the significant changes in the practitioners of Catholic theology from priests to a predominance of laypeople today who are well-trained and publish many important books and articles. The growth of the discipline of Catholic theology is one of the most important developments in the seventy-five-year history of the CTSA. As a result, the CTSA today is truly an academic society with many and diverse papers presented at its annual meetings. Academic theologians are encouraged and often even subsidized by their institutions to attend and give papers at academic societies such as the CTSA. Thus, the academic ethos had an influential role in the growth of Catholic theology in this country and in the life and work of the CTSA.

The third public that theology relates to is the broader society and the world. The Catholic tradition has always dealt with the broader society and the world. The social encyclicals beginning with Pope Leo XIII at the end of the nineteenth century used Thomistic philosophy to address the problems of the world. Vatican II and subsequent developments saw a basic connection between the gospel and the transformation of the world, thus calling for a much greater involvement of the Church in the life of the world. Vatican II's Pastoral Constitution on the Church in the Modern World (no. 1) began with the assertion: "the joys and hopes, the griefs and anxieties of this age, especially those who are poor or in any way afflicted, these too are the joys and hopes, the griefs and anxieties of the followers of Christ. Indeed, nothing genuinely human fails to raise an echo in their hearts." Justice in the World, the document of the 1971 Synod of Bishops, insists, "Action on behalf of justice and participation in the transformation of the world fully appear to us as a constitutive dimension of the preaching of the Gospel, or, in other words, of the Church's mission for the redemption of the human race and its liberation from every oppressive situation."[1]

The previous chapters of this book did not attempt to discuss every paper presented at the annual conventions of the CTSA, but the previous chapters, especially chapters 3 and 4, show how the CTSA addressed the general understanding of the role of the Church in the transformation of the world and many of the particular issues, such as poverty, racism, ecology, and people on the margins, that emerged in this time as important issues. New issues and problems are always arising and need to be addressed.

Those who attended the first meeting of the CTSA in 1946 had no idea of how Catholic theology and the CTSA would develop in the subsequent seventy-five years. We find ourselves today both reflecting on the past seventy-five years and wondering what the next seventy-five years will look like. Just as the original members in 1946, so we too cannot predict the future development of the CTSA in terms of both its internal life and the theology found in the papers at the conventions. It seems, however, that the relationship to the three publics of the Church, the academy, and the world will greatly affect how Catholic theology and the CTSA will develop.

APPENDIX A

Officers and Members of the Board of Directors

President

María Pilar Aquino	2019–2020
Paul Lakeland	2018–2019
Mary E. Hines	2017–2018
David Hollenbach	2016–2017
Bradford E. Hinze	2015–2016
Susan K. Wood	2014–2015
Richard R. Gaillardetz	2013–2014
Susan A. Ross	2012–2013
John E. Thiel	2011–2012
Mary Ann Hinsdale	2010–2011
Bryan N. Massingale	2009–2010
Terrence W. Tilley	2008–2009
Margaret O'Gara	2007–2008
Daniel Finn	2006–2007
Mary Catherine Hilkert	2005–2006
Roberto Goizueta	2004–2005
M. Shawn Copeland	2003–2004
Jon Nilson	2002–2003
Peter Phan	2001–2002

Kenneth R. Himes	2000–2001
Margaret Farley	1999–2000
Robert Schreiter	1998–1999
Mary Ann Donovan	1997–1998
Wm. Thompson-Uberuaga	1996–1997
Elizabeth Johnson	1995–1996
Roger Haight	1994–1995
Gerard S. Sloyan	1993–1994
Lisa Sowle Cahill	1992–1993
Michael J. Buckley	1991–1992
Walter H. Principe	1990–1991
Anne E. Patrick	1989–1990
John P. Boyle	1988–1989
Michael J. Scanlon	1987–1988
Monika K. Hellwig	1986–1987
Francis S. Fiorenza	1985–1986
Patrick Granfield	1984–1985
Michael Fahey	1983–1984
Bernard J. Cooke	1982–1983
Leo J. O'Donovan	1981–1982
Thomas F. O'Meara	1980–1981
William J. Hill	1979–1980
Kenan B. Osborne	1978–1979
Agnes Cunningham	1977–1978
David W. Tracy	1976–1977
Avery Dulles	1975–1976
Luke Salm	1974–1975
Richard P. McBrien	1973–1974
John H. Wright	1972–1973
Carl J. Peter	1971–1972
Richard A. McCormick	1970–1971
Charles E. Curran	1969–1970

Austin B. Vaughn	1968–1969
Walter J. Burghardt	1967–1968
Paul E. McKeever	1966–1967
Eamon R. Carroll	1965–1966
Gerald Van Ackeren	1964–1965
Richard T. Doherty	1963–1964
Ferrer Smith	1962–1963
Aloysius McDonough	1961–1962
Thomas W. Coyle	1960–1961
Lawrence J. Riley	1959–1960
Michael J. Murphy	1958–1959
John F. X. Sweeney	1957–1958
George W. Shea	1956–1957
Augustine P. Hennessy	1955–1956
William R. O'Connor	1954–1955
Gerard Yelle	1953–1954
John M. A. Fearns	1952–1953
Edmond D. Bernard	1951–1952
John J. Galvin	1950–1951
Gerard Kelly	1949–1950
Eugene M. Burke	1948–1949
James E. O'Connell	1947–1948
Francis J. Connell	1946–1947

Secretary

Hosffman Ospino	2019–
Natalie Kertes Weaver	2013–2018
M. Theresa Moser	2003–2013, 2018–2019
Mary Ann Hinsdale	1996–2003
Edward H. Konerman	1976–1996
Agnes Cunningham	1970–1976
Warren Reich	1966–1970

Vincent J. Nugent	1959–1966
Aloysius McDonough	1948–1959
Augustine P. Hennessy	1947–1948
Joseph C. Fenton	1946–1947

Treasurer

John D. Dadosky	2016–
Jozef D. Zalot	2006–2016
Roger McGrath	1993–2006
Mary E. Hines	1988–1993
George Kilcourse	1981–1988
Michael Scanlon	1975–1981
Philip D. Morris	1970–1975
Luke Salm	1959–1970
James E. Rea	1948–1959
Martin J. Healy	1947–1948
James E. Rea	1946–1947

Executive Director[1]

Mary Jane Ponyik	2012–
Dolores L. Christie	1997–2012
Joan Mueller	1996–1997
Maryanne Stevens	1994–1996
Michael J. McGinniss	1991–1994

CTSA Board Members

Meghan J. Clark	2019–2021
Timothy Matovina	2019–2021
Kevin F. Burke	2018–2020
Julie Hanlon Rubio	2018–2020

---

1. In 1976, the CTSA established the position of executive secretary with Luke Salm in the position, but this position ceased after ten years. In 1991, the CTSA established the position of executive director.

Edmund Chia	2017–2019
Michele Saracino	2017–2019
Susan Abraham	2016–2018
Mark F. Fischer	2016–2018
Catherine E. Clifford	2015–2017
Natalia M. Imperatori-Lee	2015–2017
J. Matthew Ashley	2014–2016
Mary Jo Iozzio	2014–2016
Dawn Nothwehr	2013–2015
Paulinus Odozor	2013–2015
Elizabeth T. Groppe	2012–2014
James F. Keenan	2012–2014
Kathleen McManus	2011–2013
Elena G. Procario-Foley	2011–2013
Michael E. Lee	2010–2012
Judith A. Merkle	2010–2012
Kristin E. Heyer	2009–2011
Vincent Miller	2009–2011
Nancy Pineda-Madrid	2009–2010
Miguel Díaz	2008–2009
Christine Firer Hinze	2008–2010
Stephen Bevans	2007–2009
Nancy Pineda-Madrid	2007–2009
Mary C. Boys	2006–2008
Richard R. Gaillardetz	2006–2008
Paul G. Crowley	2005–2007
Patricia Beattie Jung	2005–2007
Bryan Massingale	2004–2006
John Thiel	2004–2006
Mary Hines	2003–2005
Leo Lefebure	2003–2005
María Pilar Aquino	2002–2004
Daniel R. Finn	2002–2004

Francis Clooney	2001–2003
Thomas Shannon	2001–2003
Bradford Hinze	2000–2002
Sandra Schneiders	2000–2002
Robert Imbelli	1999–2001
Susan K. Wood	1999–2001
Anne M. Clifford	1998–2000
Roberto Goizueta	1998–2000
Diana Hayes	1997–1999
James Pambrun	1997–1999
Susan Secker	1996–1998
Jeffrey Gros	1996–1998
Terrence Tilley	1995–1997
Mary Ellen Sheehan	1995–1997
Peter Phan	1994–1996
M. Shawn Copeland	1994–1996
Robert Schreiter	1993–1995
Jon Nilson	1993–1995
Ellen Leonard	1992–1994
Kenneth Himes	1992–1994
Susan A. Ross	1991–1993
Orlando Espín	1991–1993
Matthew L. Lamb	1990–1992
Jamie T. Phelps	1990–1992
Joseph A. Bracken	1989–1991
Joann Wolski Conn	1989–1991
Mary Catherine Hilkert	1988–1990
William M. Thompson	1988–1990
Catherine Mowry LaCugna	1987–1989
Peter F. Chirico	1987–1989
Elizabeth A. Johnson	1986–1988
Roger D. Haight	1986–1988
Anne E. Patrick	1985–1987

William P. Loewe	1985–1987
Michael Fahey	1984–1985
Margaret O'Gara	1984–1986
Robert J. Daly	1984–1986
Bernard Cooke	1983–1985
Anthony R. Kosnik	1983–1985
Timothy E. O'Connell	1983–1985
Leo J. O'Donovan	1982–1984
Mary Ann Donovan	1982–1984
David Hollenbach	1982–1984
Joanne Dewart	1981–1983
Thomas F. O'Meara	1981–1983
T. Howland Sanks	1981–1983
Edward Braxton	1980–1982
Margaret Farley	1980–1982
T. Howland Sanks	1980–1982
Leo J. O'Donovan	1979–1981
Kenan B. Osborne	1979–1981
Regis Duffy	1979–1981
Frederick Crowe	1978–1980
John Boyle	1978–1980
Agnes Cunningham	1978–1980
Gregory Baum	1977–1979
Sara Butler	1977–1979
David W. Tracy	1977–1979
John Connelly	1976–1978
Michael Fahey	1976–1978
Avery Dulles	1976–1978
Francis Fiorenza	1975–1977
Suzanne Noffke	1973–1977
Luke Salm	1973–1977
David W. Tracy	1974–1976
Harry McSorley	1974–1976

Richard P. McBrien	1974–1976
Kenan B. Osborne	1973–1975
Joseph A. Komonchak	1973–1975
John H. Wright	1973–1975
Thomas F. O'Meara	1972–1974
Carl J. Peter	1972–1974
Thomas G. Dailey	1972–1974
Carl Armbruster	1971–1973
Daniel V. Flynn	1971–1973
Richard A. McCormick	1971–1973
Avery Dulles	1970–1972
Richard P. McBrien	1970–1972
Charles E. Curran	1970–1972
Luke Salm	1970–1971
Agnes Cunningham	1969–1970
Eugene Van Antwerp	1969–1971
Austin B. Vaughan	1969–1971
Thomas E. Clarke	1968–1970
George Dyer	1968–1970
Walter J. Burghardt	1968–1970
John P. Whalen	1967–1969
William G. Topmueller	1967–1969
Paul E. McKeever	1967–1969
Robert E. Hunt	1966–1968
Maurice Duchaine	1966–1968
Eamon R. Carroll	1966–1968
Gerald Van Ackeren	1965–1967
Willis J. Egan	1965–1967
Augustine Rock	1965–1967
Richard T. Doherty	1964–1966
Bonaventure H. Schwinn	1964–1966
Austin B. Vaughan	1964–1966
Ferrer Smith	1963–1965

James E. Rea	1963–1965
John H. Ziegler	1963–1965
Aloysius McDonough	1962–1964
Alban A. Maguire	1962–1964
Francis D. Costa	1962–1964
Thomas W. Coyle	1961–1963
John C. Ford	1961–1963
Martin J. Healy	1961–1963
Lawrence J. Riley	1960–1962
Gerard Owens	1960–1962
Edward F. Hanahoe	1960–1962
Michael J. Murphy	1959–1961
Forrest J. Macken	1959–1961
John A. Goodwine	1959–1961
Gerald F. Van Ackeren	1958–1960
Robert R. Masterson	1958–1960
John F. X. Sweeney	1958–1960
George W. Shea	1957–1959
Alfred Rush	1957–1959
Joseph Spitzig	1957–1959
Michael J. Murphy	1957–1958
William A. Bachmann	1956–1958
Edward J. Carney	1956–1958
Augustine P. Hennessy	1956–1958
William R. O'Connor	1955–1957
Louis E. Sullivan	1955–1957
Vincent J. Nugent	1955–1957
Gerard Yelle	1954–1956
Joseph A. M. Quigley	1954–1956
Edward F. Hanahoe	1954–1956
John M. A. Fearns	1953–1955
John F. Sweeney	1953–1955
Augustine P. Hennessey	1953–1955

J. J. McLarney	1952–1954
Edmond D. Benard	1952–1954
George W. Shea	1952–1954
Thomas J. Riley	1951–1953
John J. Galvin	1951–1953
Leonard McCann	1951–1953
John M. A. Fearns	1950–1952
Gerald Kelly	1950–1952
Martin J. Healy	1950–1952
Francis J. Connell	1949–1951
Gerard Yelle	1949–1951
Eugene M. Burke	1949–1951
James O'Connell	1948–1950
Matthew A. Schumacher	1948–1950
John J. Galvin	1948–1950
John P. Haran	1947–1949
Edward A. Wuenschel	1947–1949
Francis S. Shea	1947–1949
Joseph A. M. Quigley	1946–1948
J. Courtney Murray	1946–1948
William R. O'Connor	1946–1948
David Baier	1946–1947
Thomas Owen Martin	1946–1947
Richard D. Doherty	1946–1947

APPENDIX B

Award Recipients

The Cardinal Spellman Award[1]

Raymond E. Brown	1971
Avery Dulles	1970
Richard A. McCormick	1969
Martin R. P. McGuire	1968
John L. McKenzie	1967
Paul K. Meagher	1966
Godfrey Diekmann	1965
Barnabas M. Ahern	1964
Francis Dvornik	1963
Walter J Burghardt	1962
Cyril Vollert	1961
Johannes Quasten	1960
Juniper B. Carol	1959
Joseph C. Fenton	1958
Gerard Yelle	1957
John C. Ford	1956
Edmond D. Bernard	1955
Francis J. Connell	1954

---

1. The Cardinal·Spellman Award is the highest award given by the CTSA for distinguished contribution to theology. In 1972, Cardinal Spellman's successor chose not to give the award to the person proposed. The board of directors then changed the name of the award to the John Courtney Murray Award.

Gerald Kelly	1953
Emmanuel Doronzo	1952
William R. O'Connor	1951
John Courtney Murray	1950
Bernard J. Lonergan	1949
Eugene M. Burke	1948
William R. O'Connor	1947
John Courtney Murray	1947
Gerard Yelle	1947
Emmanuel Doronzo	1947
Francis J. Connell	1947

John Courtney Murray Award

James F. Keenan	2019
M. Shawn Copeland	2018
Francis X. Clooney	2017
Orlando O. Espín	2016
Joseph A. Komonchak	2015
John Pawlikowski	2014
Anne E. Patrick	2013
Terrence W. Tilley	2012
James A. Coriden	2011
Peter C. Phan	2010
David Bakewell Burrell	2009
Lisa Sowle Cahill	2008
Virgilio Elizondo	2007
Sandra M. Schneiders	2006
Robert Schreiter	2005
Elizabeth A. Johnson	2004
Michael Fahey	2003
Kenan Osborne	2002
Agnes Cunningham	2001
Michael J. Buckley	2000

Ladislas Orsy	1999
David Hollenbach	1998
Anne E. Carr	1997
David N. Power	1996
John T. & Denise Carmody	1995
Francis A. Sullivan	1994
Kilian P. McDonnell	1993
Margaret A. Farley	1992
Thomas F. O'Meara	1991
Frederick R. McManus	1990
Patrick Granfield	1989
Richard J. Sklba	1988
Walter H. Principe	1987
Gregory Baum	1986
Zachary J. Hayes	1985
Monika K. Hellwig	1984
William J. Hill	1983
George J. Dyer	1982
Gerard S. Sloyan	1981
David W. Tracy	1980
Bernard Cooke	1979
Edward Kilmartin	1978
Frederick E. Crowe	1977
Richard. P. McBrien	1976
Carl J. Peter	1975
George H. Tavard	1974
Bernard J. F. Lonergan	1973
Charles E. Curran	1972

Ann O'Hara Graff Memorial Award[2]

Mary Rose D'Angelo	2019

---

2. The Women's Consultation in Constructive Theology gives the Ann O'Hara Graff Memorial Award to a woman scholar member of the CTSA.

Nancy Pineda-Madrid	2018
Margaret Farley	2017
Elizabeth Johnson	2016
Patricia Beattie Jung	2015
M. Shawn Copeland	2014
Mary C. Boys	2013
M. Catherine Hilkert	2012
Joann Wolski Conn	2011
Jamie Phelps	2010
Anne Patrick	2009
Barbara Hilkert Andolsen	2008
Anne Carr	2007
María Pilar Aquino	2006
Gaile Pohlhaus	2005
Ellen Leonard	2004
Monika Hellwig	2003
Mary Ann Hinsdale	2002
Susan Ross	2001
Diana Hayes	2000
Regina Coll	1999
Joan Timmerman	1998

Catherine Mowry Lacugna Award[3]

Antonio Eduardo Alonso	2019
Elizabeth Antus	2018
Judith Gruber	2017
Benjamin Maurice Durheim &	
David Turnbloom	2016
Nichole Marie Flores	2015
Michael Peppard	2014
Christiana Z. Peppard	2013

---

3. The CTSA gives the Catherine Mowry Lacugna Award to new scholars for the best academic essay in Catholic theology.

APPENDIX B

Anna Harrison	2012
Kimberly Baker	2011
Stephen Bullivant	2010
Christopher Pramuk	2009
Dominic Doyle	2008
Laura Grimes	2007
Laura M. Taylor	2006
Gemma Tulud Cruz	2005

NOTES

CHAPTER 1: THE ORIGINS OF THE CATHOLIC THEOLOGICAL SOCIETY OF AMERICA

1. G. F. McLean, "American Catholic Philosophical Association," *New Catholic Encyclopedia* (New York: McGraw Hill, 1967), 1:398.

2. *Res Philosophica* at www.resphilosophica.org.

3. E. J. Ross, "American Catholic Sociological Society," *New Catholic Encyclopedia* 1, 399; Association for the Sociology of Religion at www.sociologyofreligion.com; Thomas F. Divine, "The Origins of the Catholic Economic Association," *Review of Social Economy* 2 (1944): 102–3; Association for Social Economics at www.socialeconomics.org.

4. Charles E. Curran, *Catholic Moral Theology in the United States: A History* (Washington, DC: Georgetown University Press, 2008), 39.

5. Edward J. Power, *Catholic Higher Education in America: A History* (New York: Appleton-Century-Crofts, 1972), 36–45.

6. Power, *Catholic Higher Education*, 302–4.

7. Philip Gleason, "American Catholic Higher Education: A Historical Perspective," in *The Shape of Catholic Higher Education*, ed. Robert Hassenger (Chicago: University of Chicago Press, 1967), 35–38.

8. Power, *Catholic Higher Education*, 3.

9. Very Reverend Hunter Guthrie, "Presidential Address," in *Tradition and Prospect: The Inauguration of the Very Rev. Hunter*

Guthrie, SJ, 1949 (Washington, DC: Georgetown University Press, 1949), 70–74.

10. Philip Gleason, *Keeping the Faith: American Catholicism Past and Present* (Notre Dame, IN: University of Notre Dame Press, 1987), 166–72.

11. See, e.g., Etienne Gilson, ed., *The Church Speaks to the Modern World: The Social Teachings of Leo XIII* (Garden City, NY: Doubleday Image Book, 1954):

12. Philip Gleason, *Contending with Modernity: Catholic Higher Education in the Twentieth Century* (New York: Oxford University Press, 1995), 6.

13. Sandra Yocum Mize, *Joining the Revolution in Theology: The College Theology Society 1954–2004* (Lanham, MD: Littlefield, 2007), 31–61.

14. Andrew M. Greeley, *From Backwater to Mainstream: A Profile of Catholic Higher Education* (New York: McGraw-Hill, 1969).

15. "Land O'Lakes Statement," in *The Catholic University: A Modern Appraisal*, ed. Neil G. McCluskey (Notre Dame, IN: University of Notre Dame Press, 1970), 336–37.

16. Joseph M. White, *The Diocesan Seminary in the United States: A History from the 1780s to the Present* (Notre Dame, IN: University of Notre Dame Press, 1989).

17. White, *Diocesan Seminary*, 189–208, 318–35.

18. The following paragraphs are based on Joseph Clifford Fenton, "The Foundation and Progress of the Society," in *Proceedings of the Foundational Meeting 1946*, 5–12; "The Constitution of the Society," *Proceedings 1946*, 13–20; Eugene M. Burke, "Appendix B: A Personal Memoir on the Origins of the CTSA," *Proceedings 1980*, 337–45; Eugene M. Burke, "Appendix II: A Personal Memoir; Part Two," *Proceedings 1984*, 235–41.

19. This and all subsequent references to the *Proceedings* of the annual meeting will appear in the text and will simply give the year of the *Proceedings* followed by the pages.

20. White, *Diocesan Seminary*, 365–80.

21. E.g., Severinus Gonzalez, *De Gratia Christi*, in *Sacrae Theologiae Summa*, vol. 3 (Madrid: Biblioteca de Autores Cristianos, 1956), 494–500.

22. For a negative evaluation of the thesis approach used at that time, see Philip A. Egan, *Philosophy and Catholic Theology: A Primer* (Collegeville, MN: Liturgical Press, 2009).

CHAPTER 2: THE CATHOLIC THEOLOGICAL SOCIETY OF AMERICA, 1947–1970

1. Albert C. Pierce, *Beyond One Man: Catholic University April 17–24, 1967* (N.p.: Anawim, 1967), 59–60.

2. Philip D. Morris, ed., *Metropolis: Christian Presence and Responsibility* (Notre Dame, IN: Fides, 1967).

3. Charles E. Curran and George J. Dyer, eds., *Shared Responsibility in the Local Church* (Chicago: Chicago Studies, 1970).

4. Rosemary Rodgers, *A History of the College Theology Society* (Villanova, PA: College Theology Society, 1983), 4.

5. Robert J. Wister, "CTSA Membership Analysis," *Proceedings 1995*, 301. Wister was the archivist of the CTSA and commissioned to write the history. In correspondence with me, he pointed out that the archives of the CTSA were at Theological College of CUA in Washington. The building, however, was being renovated, and he could not have access at that time to the archives. In the 1995 proceedings, he published four very short reports: "CTSA Firsts," "CTSA Presidents," "CTSA Award Winners," and "CTSA Membership Analysis."

6. Christopher J. Kauffman, "The Neutralist Layman," *Continuum* 1, no. 3 (Autumn 1963): 411–12.

7. Marirose Osborne, "Speaker Remembers College's Graduate School of Theology," at https://ndsmcobserver.com/2019/03/speaker-remembers-colleges-graduate-school-of-theology. The speaker was Sandra Yocum Mize, the author of the history of the College Theology Society.

8. Charles E. Curran, *The Development of Moral Theology: Five Strands* (Washington, DC: Georgetown University Press, 2013), 48–54.

9. J. Leon Hooper, *The Ethics of Discourse: The Social Philosophy of John Courtney Murray* (Washington, DC: Georgetown University Press, 1986), 121–56.

10. Gerald Fogarty, *American Catholic Biblical Scholarship: A History from the Early Republic to Vatican II* (San Francisco: Harper & Row, 1989), 27.

11. For the attacks on Brown and his reaction, see Donald Senior, *Raymond E. Brown and the Catholic Biblical Renewal* (New York: Paulist Press, 2018), 28.

12. Anne E. Carr, "Mary and the Mystery of the Church: Vatican Council II," in *Mary According to Women*, ed. Carol Frances Jegen (Kansas City, MO: Leaven Press, 1985), 5–32.

13. Francis L. Broderick, *Right Reverend New Dealer* (New York: Macmillan, 1963), 117, 262.

14. Joseph T. Leonard, *Theology and Race Relations* (Milwaukee: Bruce, 1963). This was originally a doctoral dissertation written at CUA under the direction of Francis J. Connell.

CHAPTER 3: THE CATHOLIC THEOLOGICAL SOCIETY OF AMERICA, 1971–1995

1. "Congregation for the Doctrine of the Faith on John McNeill, *The Church and the Homosexual*, Summer 1978," in *Dialogue about Catholic Sexual Teaching*, ed. Charles E. Curran and Richard A. McCormick, Readings in Moral Theology 8 (New York: Paulist Press, 1983), 91–97.

2. Kenneth A. Briggs, "Catholics Criticize a Book on Sexuality," *New York Times*, November 17, 1977, 19.

3. Congregation for the Doctrine of the Faith, "Observations about the Book, *Human Sexuality: A Study Commissioned by the Catholic Theological Society of America*, Rev. Anthony Kosnik, Editor," July 13, 1979, http://www.vatican.va/roman_curia/congregations/cfaith/documents/rc_con_cfaith_doc_19790713_mons-quinn_en.html.

4.   Fellowship of Catholic Scholars, "About Us," at https://www
.catholicscholars.org/aboutus.php.

5.   Leo J. O'Donovan, ed., *Cooperation between Theologians and the Ecclesiastical Magisterium: A Report of the Joint Committee of the Canon Law Society of America and the Catholic Theological Society of America* (Washington, DC: Canon Law Society of America, 1982).

6.   For more on the Monsour case, see Helen Marie Burns, "The Experience of the Sisters of Mercy of the Union in Public Offices," in *Authority, Community, and Conflict,* ed. Madonna Kolbenschlag (Kansas City, MO: Sheed and Ward, 1986), 1–19.

7.   Ari L. Goldman, "Book's Popularity Tests the Vatican," *New York Times,* November 29, 1984, 23; Raymond G. Hunthausen, "Archbishop Hunthausen Withdraws Imprimatur," *Origins* 14 (1984): 15–16.

8.   Charles E. Curran, *Loyal Dissent: Memoir of a Catholic Theologian* (Washington, DC: Georgetown University Press, 2006), 107–32.

9.   For the CUA process mentioned in this paragraph, see Curran, *Loyal Dissent,* 143–49.

10.   Curran, *Loyal Dissent,* 153–59.

11.   "Theologians in Europe Challenge Pope's Conservative Leadership," *New York Times,* July 14, 1989, 1ff..

12.   "Profession of Faith," in *Report of the Catholic Theological Society Committee on the Profession of Faith and the Oath of Fidelity* (Catholic Theological Society of America, April 15, 1990), 123.

13.   *Report,* 116.

14.   "Do Not Extinguish the Spirit," *Origins* 20 (1990–91): 463–67.

15.   Congregation for the Doctrine of the Faith, "Note on the Book by Fr. André Guindon, OMI, *The Sexual Creators: An Ethical Proposal for Concerned Christians,*" January 31, 1992, http://www.vatican
.va/roman_curia/congregations/cfaith/documents/rc_con_cfaith_doc
_19920131_book-guindon_en.html.

16.   Karl Rahner, "Toward a Fundamental Theological Interpretation of Vatican II," *Theological Studies* 40 (1979): 716–27.

17.   Lonergan Links at https://bclonergan.org/lonergan-links.

18.   Bernard J. F. Lonergan, *Method in Theology* (New York: Herder and Herder, 1972).

CHAPTER 4: THE CATHOLIC THEOLOGICAL SOCIETY OF AMERICA, 1996–2020

1. www.academyofcatholictheology.org.

2. John P. Boyle, *Church Teaching Authority: Historical and Theological Studies* (Notre Dame, IN: University of Notre Dame Press, 1995), 174.

3. United States Conference of Catholic Bishops, "Guidelines Concerning the Academic Mandate," June 15, 2001, https://www.usccb.org/committees/catholic-education/guidelines-concerning-academic-mandatum.

4. "Land O'Lakes Statement," in *The Catholic University: A Modern Appraisal*, ed. Neil G. McCluskey (Notre Dame, IN: University of Notre Dame Press, 1970), 336–37.

5. Jason King, "Review Essay on Catholic Higher Education: After *Ex Corde Ecclesiae*," *Journal of Moral Theology* 4, no. 2 (2015): 167.

6. Congregation for the Doctrine of the Faith, "Notification on the Book *Jesus Symbol of God*, by Father Roger Haight SJ," December 13, 2004, http://www.vatican.va/roman_curia/congregations/cfaith/documents/rc_con_cfaith_doc_20041213_notification-fr-haight_en.html.

7. John L. Allen, "Rome Orders Roger Haight to Stop Teaching, Publishing," *National Catholic Reporter*, January 5, 2009, https://www.ncronline.org/news/rome-orders-roger-haight-stop-teaching-publishing.

8. "Vatican Critiques Book by Mercy Sister Margaret Farley," USCCB News Release, June 4, 2012.

9. Bradford Hinze, "A Decade of Disciplining Theologians," *Horizons* 37, no. 1 (2010): 92–126.

10. Laurie Goodstein and Rachel Donadio, "Vatican Scolds Nun for Book on Sexuality," *New York Times*, June 4, 2012.

11. *Interrupting White Privilege: Catholic Theologians Break the Silence*, ed. Laurie M. Cassidy and Alex Mikulich (Maryknoll, NY: Orbis Books, 2007).

CONCLUSION

1. Synod of Bishops, 1971, *Justitia in Mundo*, in *Catholic Social Thought: The Documentary Heritage*, ed. David J. O'Brien and Thomas A. Shannon, exp. ed. (Maryknoll, NY: Orbis Books, 2010), 306.

INDEX